Coaching Youth Baseball

HUMAN KINETICS

Library of Congress Cataloging-in-Publication Data

Names: Babe Ruth League, author.
Title: Coaching youth baseball / Babe Ruth League.
Description: Champaign, IL : Human Kinetics, [2020]
Identifiers: LCCN 2018039834 (print) | LCCN 2018055167 (ebook) | ISBN
    9781492589303 (epub) | ISBN 9781492589297 (PDF) | ISBN 9781450453400
    (print)
Subjects: LCSH: Youth league baseball--Coaching. | Baseball for
    children--Coaching.
Classification: LCC GV880.65 (ebook) | LCC GV880.65 .B34 2020 (print) | DDC
    796.357/62--dc23

LC record available at https://lccn.loc.gov/2018039834

ISBN: 978-1-4504-5340-0 (print)

The web addresses cited in this text were current as of November 2018, unless otherwise noted.

Managing Editor: Julie Marx Goodreau
Copyeditor: Anne Rumery
Permissions Manager: Martha Gullo
Graphic Designer: Julie L. Denzer
Cover Designer: Keri Evans
Cover Design Associate: Susan Rothermel Allen
Photograph (cover): © Human Kinetics
Photographs (interior): Gregg Henness/© Human Kinetics
Photo Production Coordinator: Amy Rose
Photo Production Manager: Jason Allen
Senior Art Manager: Kelly Hendren
Illustrations: © Human Kinetics, unless otherwise noted
Printer: Versa Press

Copies of this book are available at special discounts for bulk purchase for sales promotions, premiums, fund-raising, or educational use. Special editions or book excerpts can also be created to specifications. For details, contact the Special Sales Manager at Human Kinetics.

Printed in the United States of America   10 9 8 7 6 5 4 3 2 1

The paper in this book is certified under a sustainable forestry program.

Human Kinetics
P.O. Box 5076
Champaign, IL 61825-5076
Website: www.HumanKinetics.com

In the United States, email info@hkusa.com or call 800-747-4457.
In Canada, email info@hkcanada.com.
In the United Kingdom/Europe, email hk@hkeurope.com.

For information about Human Kinetics' coverage in other areas of the world,
please visit our website: **www.HumanKinetics.com**

E5947

⚾ Contents

Drill Finder

Key to Diagrams

(P)   Pitcher

(C)   Catcher

CO   Coach

(1B)   1st base player

(2B)   2nd base player

(3B)   3rd base player

(SS)   Shortstop

(LF)   Left fielder

(CF)   Center fielder

(RF)   Right fielder

B   Batter

R   Runner

F   Fielder, general

———→   Path of runner/fielder

- - - - →   Path of hit/tossed ball

··············►   Path of throw

Stepping Into Coaching

If you are like most youth league coaches, you have probably been recruited from the ranks of concerned parents, sport enthusiasts, or community volunteers. Like many rookie and veteran coaches, you probably have had little formal instruction on how to coach. But when the call went out for coaches to assist with your local Babe Ruth League program, you answered because you like children and enjoy baseball, and perhaps because you wanted to be involved in a worthwhile community activity.

Making the decision to become a coach carries a tremendous amount of responsibility. At the youngest ages, coaches serve as authority figures, models of behavior, and even heroes to the kids on their teams. They have an opportunity to create a fun and positive experience that fuels an interest in the game that can last a lifetime. As the players get older, coaches have the ability to affect the lives of their players on a different level, passing on life lessons that make a lasting impression as the players move forward in baseball and school. These lessons can be powerful, carrying over well into adulthood and eventually getting passed down to future generations of Babe Ruth League participants.

Like many volunteers, you may not know everything there is to know about baseball or about how to work with children. *Coaching Youth Baseball* presents the basics of coaching baseball effectively. To start, we look at your responsibilities and what's involved in being a coach. We also talk about what to do when your own child is on the team you coach, and we examine five tools for being an effective coach.

Whether you're functioning as a manager, coach, or just an interested parent, the players on your team will look to you for guidance and examples of good leadership. The bulk of their training will come from the managers and coaches, since these are the individuals who have the most direct contact with the players. But when it comes to general guidance and leadership examples, every manager and coach has an obligation to teach beyond the rules and basics of the game. They have an obligation to their players to provide them with the best possible instruction and leadership of which they are capable. So, in terms of general guidance and leadership, your role is extremely important. Be prepared for this responsibility!

Your Responsibilities As a Babe Ruth League Coach

Coaching at all levels involves much more than making out the lineup, hitting fungoes, or coaching third base. Coaching involves accepting the tremendous responsibility you face when parents put their children into your care. As a Babe Ruth League coach, you'll be called on to do the following:

1. Provide a safe physical environment.

The safety and security of our players, volunteers, and spectators has always been a major consideration of Babe Ruth League, Inc. Playing baseball holds inherent risks, but as a coach you're responsible for regularly inspecting the fields and equipment used for practice and competition (see Facilities and Equipment Checklist at the end of chapter 4).

2. Communicate in a positive way.

As you can already see, you have a lot to communicate. You'll communicate not only with your players and their parents, but also with the coaching staff, umpires, administrators, and others. Communicate in a way that is positive and that demonstrates that you have the best interests of the players at heart (see chapter 2 for more information). Babe Ruth League coaches who clearly explain all team rules and coaching philosophies are off to a good start in developing team chemistry.

3. Teach the fundamental skills of baseball.

When teaching the game to young Babe Ruth Leaguers, *fun* should be the number one goal. If the kids don't have fun, they won't continue to play when they are older. Therefore, you want to be sure that your players have fun while learning the basics. We ask that you help and encourage all players to be the best they can be by creating a fun, yet productive, practice environment. To help you do this, we'll show you an innovative games approach to teaching and practicing the skills young players need to know—an approach that kids thoroughly enjoy (see chapter 5 for more information). Additionally, to help your players improve their skills, you need to have a sound understanding of offensive and defensive skills. We'll provide information to assist you in gaining that understanding (see chapters 7, 8, and 9 for more information).

4. Teach the rules of baseball.

Introduce the rules of baseball and incorporate them into individual instruction (see chapter 3 for more information). Many rules can be taught in practice, including offensive rules (such as the definition of the strike zone, rules related to the baseline, and when sliding is mandatory) as well as defensive rules (such as the force play, the balk rule, and obstruction). You should plan to review the rules any time an opportunity naturally arises in practices.

5. Direct players in competition.

Your responsibilities include determining starting lineups and a substitution plan, relating appropriately to umpires and to opposing coaches and players, and making sound tactical decisions during games (see chapter 10 for more information on coaching during games). Remember that the focus is not on winning at all costs but on coaching your kids to compete well, do their best, improve their baseball skills, and strive to win within the rules.

6. Help your players become fit and value fitness for a lifetime.

We want you to help your players be fit so they can play baseball safely and successfully. We also want your players to learn to become fit on their own, understand the value of fitness, and enjoy training. Thus, we ask you not to make them do push-ups or run laps for punishment. Make it fun to get fit for baseball, and make it fun to play baseball so that they'll stay fit for a lifetime.

    7. **Help young people develop character.**

Character development includes learning, caring, being honest and respectful, and taking responsibility. These intangible qualities are no less important to teach than the skill of hitting the baseball. We ask you to teach these values to players by demonstrating and encouraging behaviors that express these values at all times. For example, in teaching good team defense, stress to young players the importance of learning their assignments, helping their teammates, playing within the rules, showing respect for their opponents, and understanding that they are responsible for having a role in every play—even though they may not be recognized individually for their efforts.

    These are your responsibilities as a Babe Ruth League coach. Remember that every player is an individual. You must provide a wholesome environment in which every player has the opportunity to learn how to play the game without fear while having fun and enjoying the overall Babe Ruth League experience.

Coaching Your Own Child

Coaching a Babe Ruth League team can be difficult. When your own kid plays on the squad, this task can become even more complicated. Many coaches are parents, but the two roles should not be confused. As a parent, you are responsible only for yourself and your child, but as a coach you are also responsible for the organization, all the players on the team, and communications with their parents. Because of this additional responsibility, your behavior on the baseball field will be different from your behavior at home, and your child may not understand why.

    For example, imagine the confusion of a young boy who is the center of his parents' attention at home but is barely noticed by his father (who is the coach of his Babe Ruth team) in the sport setting. Or consider the mixed signals received by a young player whose skill is constantly evaluated by a coach (who is also his mother) who otherwise rarely comments on her son's activities. You need to explain to your child your new responsibilities and how they will affect your relationship when coaching. Take the following steps to avoid problems in coaching your own child:

- Get his input first. Ask your child if he wants you to coach the team.
- Explain why you want to be involved with his Babe Ruth team.
- Discuss with your child how your interactions will change when you take on the role of coach at practices or games.
- Limit your coaching behavior to when you are in the coaching role.

- Avoid parenting during practice or game situations to keep your role clear in your child's mind.
- Reaffirm your love for your child, irrespective of his performance on the baseball field.

COACHING TIP Coaches who work with their own children, especially when the child is under 12 years of age, have to walk a delicate line when praising or criticizing their own child in front of the team. Be careful what you say about your own child in front of your Babe Ruth team when you go over the pluses and minuses of a previous game or the day's practice. Because players are so conscious of the coach–child relationship, it might be best not to highlight either the positives or the negatives of your child's play at practice or games. Instead, you can save your comments for the ride home in the car or maybe make a brief remark when others aren't present.

Five Tools of an Effective Coach

Have you purchased the traditional coaching tools—things such as whistles, coaching clothes, sport shoes, and a clipboard? They'll help you in the act of coaching, but to be successful, you'll need five other tools that cannot be bought. These tools are available only through self-examination and hard work; they're easy to remember with the acronym COACH:

C	Comprehension
O	Outlook
A	Affection
C	Character
H	Humor

Comprehension

Comprehension of the rules and skills of baseball is required. You must understand the basic elements of the sport. To improve your comprehension of baseball, take the following steps:

- Read about the rules of baseball in chapter 3 of this book.
- Read about the fundamental skills of baseball in chapters 7, 8, and 9.
- Read additional baseball coaching books, including those available from Human Kinetics.
- Contact Babe Ruth League headquarters.
- Attend a district or state Babe Ruth League coaching clinic.

- Talk with more experienced Babe Ruth League coaches.
- Observe local college, high school, and other Babe Ruth League games.
- Watch baseball games on television.

In addition to having baseball knowledge, you must implement proper training and safety methods so that your players can participate with little risk of injury. Even then, injuries may occur. And more often than not, you'll be the first person responding to your players' injuries, so be sure you understand the basic emergency care procedures described in chapter 4. Also, read in that chapter how to handle more serious sport injury situations.

Outlook

This coaching tool refers to your perspective and goals—what you seek as a coach. The most common coaching objectives are to (1) have fun; (2) help players develop their physical, mental, and social skills; and (3) strive to win. Thus, your outlook involves your priorities, your planning, and your vision for the future. See Assessing Your Priorities to learn more about the priorities you set for yourself as a coach.

Babe Ruth League, Inc. agrees with Human Kinetics' Coach Education motto, which will help you keep your outlook in line with the best interests of the kids on your team. It summarizes in four words all you need to remember when establishing your coaching priorities:

Athletes First, Winning Second

This motto recognizes that striving to win is an important, even vital, part of sports. But it emphatically states that no efforts in striving to win should be made at the expense of the athletes' well-being, development, and enjoyment. Take the following actions to better define your outlook:

- With the members of your coaching staff, determine your priorities for the season.
- Prepare for situations that may challenge your priorities.
- Set goals for yourself and your players that are consistent with your priorities.
- Plan how you and your players can best attain your goals.
- Review your goals frequently to be sure that you are staying on track.

Affection

Another vital tool you will want to have in your coaching kit is a genuine concern for the young people you coach. This requires having a passion for kids, a desire to share with them your enjoyment and knowledge of baseball, and the patience

Assessing Your Priorities

Even though all coaches focus on competition, we want you to focus on *positive competition*—keeping the pursuit of victory in perspective by making decisions that, first, are in the best interest of the players, and second, will help to win the game.

So, how do you know if your outlook and priorities are in order? Here's a little test:

1. Which situation would you be most proud of?
   a. *Knowing that each participant enjoyed playing baseball*
   b. *Seeing that all players improved their baseball skills*
   c. *Winning the league championship*
2. Which statement best reflects your thoughts about sport?
   a. *If it isn't fun, don't do it.*
   b. *Everyone should learn something every day.*
   c. *Sport isn't fun if you don't win.*
3. How would you like your players to remember you?
   a. *As a coach who was fun to play for*
   b. *As a coach who provided a good base of fundamental skills*
   c. *As a coach who had a winning record*
4. Which would you most like to hear a parent of a player on your Babe Ruth team say?
   a. *Josh really had a good time playing baseball this year.*
   b. *Josh learned some important lessons playing baseball this year.*
   c. *Josh played on the first-place baseball team this year.*
5. Which of the following would be the most rewarding moment of your season?
   a. *Having your team want to continue playing, even after practice is over*
   b. *Seeing one of your players finally master the skill of fielding a ground ball and throwing accurately to the right base*
   c. *Winning the league championship*

Look over your answers. If you most often selected "a" responses, then having fun is most important to you. A majority of "b" answers suggests that skill development is what attracts you to coaching. And if "c" was your most frequent response, winning is top on your list of coaching priorities. If your priorities are in order, your players' well-being will take precedence over your team's win–loss record every time.

and understanding that allow all your players to grow from their involvement with the Babe Ruth League program. You can demonstrate your affection and patience in many ways, including the following:

- Make an effort to get to know each player on your Babe Ruth team.
- Treat each player as an individual.
- Empathize with players trying to learn new and difficult skills.
- Treat players as you would like to be treated under similar circumstances.
- Control your emotions.
- Show your enthusiasm for being involved with your Babe Ruth team.
- Keep an upbeat tempo and positive tone in all of your communications.

COACHING TIP All Babe Ruth League players, especially in the younger divisions, need to feel that their coach cares about them. Too many times coaches talk to the whole team and think that's adequate communication. Babe Ruth coaches should devote equal time to each team member, which makes every player feel like an integral part of the team. You should take time to talk to each of your players individually at least once a week. A good way to make sure you do this is to carry a card listing all your players' names on it in your back pocket at all times. When you talk to a player, check off the name. At the end of a week, verify that all the names have been checked off.

Character

The fact that you have decided to serve as a Babe Ruth League coach probably means that you think participation in the game is important. But whether or not that participation develops character in your players depends as much on you as it does on the sport itself. How can you help your players build character?

Having good character means modeling appropriate behaviors for baseball and life. That means more than just saying the right things. What you say and what you do must match. There is no place in coaching for the "Do as I say, not as I do" philosophy. Challenge, support, encourage, and reward every youngster, and your players will be more likely to accept, even celebrate, their differences. Be in control before, during, and after all practices and games. And don't be afraid to admit that you were wrong. No one is perfect!

Each member of your coaching staff should consider the following steps to becoming a good role model:

- Take stock of your strengths and weaknesses.
- Build on your strengths.

- Set goals for yourself to improve on those areas that you don't want to see copied by your players.
- If you slip up, apologize to your team and to yourself. You'll do better next time.

Humor

Humor is an often-overlooked coaching tool. It means having the ability to laugh at yourself and with your players during practices and games. Nothing helps balance the seriousness of a skill session like a chuckle or two. And a sense of humor puts in perspective the many mistakes your players will make. So don't get upset over each miscue or respond negatively to erring players. Allow your players and yourself to enjoy the ups, and don't dwell on the downs. Here are some tips for injecting humor and fun into your practices:

- Make practices fun by including a variety of activities.
- Keep all players involved in games and skill practices.
- Consider laughter by your players to be a sign of enjoyment, not of waning discipline.
- Smile!

Communicating As a Coach

2

In chapter 1, you learned about the tools you need for coaching: comprehension, outlook, affection, character, and humor. These are essentials for effective coaching; without them, you'd have a difficult time getting started. But none of the tools will work if you don't know how to use them with your players—and this requires skillful communication. This chapter examines what communication is and how you can become a more effective communicator.

What Is Involved in Communication

Coaches often mistakenly believe that communication occurs only when instructing players to do something, but verbal commands are only a small part of the communication process. In fact, more than half of what is communicated is done so nonverbally. So remember when you are coaching: Actions speak louder than words.

Communication in its simplest form involves two people: a sender and a receiver. The sender transmits the message verbally, through facial expressions, and possibly through body language. Once the message is sent, the receiver must receive it and, optimally, understand it. A receiver who fails to pay attention or listen will miss part, if not all, of the message.

Sending Effective Messages

Young athletes often have little understanding of the rules and skills of baseball and probably even less confidence in their ability to play the game. So, they need accurate, understandable, and supportive messages to help them along. That's why your verbal and nonverbal messages are important.

Verbal Messages

"Sticks and stones may break my bones, but words will never hurt me" isn't true. Spoken words can have a strong and long-lasting effect. And coaches' words are particularly influential because youngsters place great importance on what coaches say. Perhaps you, like many former youth sport participants, have a difficult time remembering much of anything you were told by your elementary school teachers, but you can probably still recall several specific things your coaches at that level said to you. Such is the lasting effect of a coach's comments to a player.

Whether you are correcting misbehavior, teaching a player how to catch a fly ball, or praising a player for good effort, you should consider a number of things when sending a message verbally:

- Be positive and honest.
- State it clearly and simply.

- Say it loud enough, then say it again.
- Be consistent.

Be Positive and Honest

Nothing turns people off like hearing someone nag all the time, and players react similarly to a coach who gripes constantly. Kids particularly need encouragement because they often doubt their ability to perform in a sport. So, look for and tell your players what they did well.

But don't cover up poor or incorrect play with rosy words of praise. Kids know all too well when they've erred, and no cheerfully expressed cliché can undo their mistakes. If you fail to acknowledge players' errors, your players will think you are a phony.

An effective way to correct a performance error is to first point out the part of the skill that the player performed correctly. Then explain—in a positive manner—the error that the player made and show him the correct way to do it. Finish by encouraging the player and emphasizing the correct performance.

Be sure not to follow a positive statement with the word *but*. For example, you shouldn't say, "You're the fastest runner on the team, Eric, but if you didn't get such a slow start, you wouldn't get thrown out as much." This causes many kids to ignore the positive statement and focus on the negative one. Instead, you should say something like, "You're the fastest runner on the team, Eric. Tomorrow in practice we're going to work on how to get a better jump on the pitcher. That was much better. Way to go."

State It Clearly and Simply

Positive and honest messages are good, but only if expressed directly in words your players understand. Beating around the bush is ineffective and inefficient. And if you ramble, your players will miss the point of your message and probably lose interest. Here are some tips for saying things clearly:

- Organize your thoughts before speaking to your players.
- Know your subject as completely as possible.
- Explain things thoroughly, but don't bore your players with long-winded monologues.
- Use language your players can understand, and be consistent in your terminology. However, avoid trying to be hip by using their age group's slang.

COACHING TIP Remember, terms that you are familiar with and understand may be completely foreign to your players, especially younger players or beginners. You may need to use demonstrations with the players so they can "see" the term and how it relates to the game of baseball.

Say It Loud Enough, Then Say It Again

Talk to your team in a voice that all members can hear. A crisp, vigorous voice commands attention and respect; garbled and weak speech is tuned out. It's okay and, in fact, appropriate to soften your voice when speaking to a player individually about a personal problem. But most of the time your messages will be for all your players to hear, so make sure they can! An enthusiastic voice also motivates players and tells them you enjoy being their coach. A word of caution, however: Avoid dominating the setting with a booming voice that distracts attention from players' performances.

Sometimes what you say, even if stated loudly and clearly, won't sink in the first time. This may be particularly true when young players hear words they don't understand. To avoid boring repetition and still get your message across, you can say the same thing in a slightly different way. For instance, you might first tell your players, "Don't pull your head out on your swing!" If they don't appear to understand, you might say, "Keep your front shoulder pointed at the ball when you start your swing." The second form of the message may get through to players who missed it the first time around.

Be Consistent

People often say things in ways that imply a different message. For example, a touch of sarcasm added to the words "Way to go!" sends an entirely different message than the words themselves suggest. You should avoid sending mixed messages. Keep the tone of your voice consistent with the words you use. And don't say something one day and contradict it the next; players will get their wires crossed. You also want to keep your terminology consistent. Many baseball terms describe the same or similar skills. One coach may use the term "push off the rubber" to describe how a pitcher should get his momentum going toward home plate, while another coach may tell the pitchers to "drive your front hip home!" Although both are correct, to be consistent as a staff, the coaches of a team should agree on all terms before the start of the season and then stay with them.

Nonverbal Messages

Just as you should be consistent in the tone of voice and words you use, you should also keep your verbal and nonverbal messages consistent. An extreme example of failing to do this would be shaking your head, indicating disapproval, while at the same time telling a player "Nice try." Which is the player to believe, your gesture or your words?

Messages can be sent nonverbally in several ways. Facial expressions and body language are just two of the more obvious forms of nonverbal signals that can help you when you coach. Keep in mind that as a coach you need to be a teacher first, and any action that detracts from the message you are trying to convey should be avoided.

Facial Expressions

The look on a person's face is the quickest clue to what the person thinks or feels. Your players know this, so they will study your face, looking for a sign that will tell them more than the words you say. Don't try to fool them by putting on a happy or blank "mask." They'll see through it, and you'll lose credibility.

Serious, stone-faced expressions provide no cues to kids who want to know how they are performing. When faced with this, kids will just assume you're unhappy or disinterested. Don't be afraid to smile. A smile from a coach can give a great boost to an unsure player. Plus, a smile lets your players know that you are happy coaching them. But don't overdo it, or your players won't be able to tell when you are genuinely pleased by something they've done or when you are just putting on a smiling face.

Body Language

What would your players think you were feeling if you came to practice slouched over, with your head down and your shoulders slumped? Would they think you were tired, bored, or unhappy? What would they think you were feeling if you watched them during a game with your hands on your hips, your jaws clenched, and your face reddened? Would they think you were upset with them, disgusted at an official, or mad at a fan? Probably some or all of these things would enter your players' minds. And none is the impression you want your players to have of you. That's why you should carry yourself in a pleasant, confident, and vigorous manner.

Physical contact can also be a very important use of body language. A handshake, a pat on the head, an arm around the shoulder, and even a big hug are effective ways to show approval, concern, affection, and joy to your players. Youngsters are especially in need of this type of nonverbal message. Keep within the obvious moral and legal limits, of course, but don't be reluctant to touch your players, sending a message that can only be expressed in that way.

COACHING TIP As a Babe Ruth coach, you need to be aware of your body language. You must ensure that the players are translating it correctly and that you are providing a good example for your players to model.

Improving Your Receiving Skills

Now let's examine the other half of the communication process: receiving messages. Too often very good senders are very poor receivers of messages. But as a Babe Ruth coach of young players, you must be able to fulfill both roles effectively.

The requirements for receiving messages are quite simple, but receiving skills are perhaps less satisfying and therefore underdeveloped compared to sending skills. People seem to enjoy hearing themselves talk more than they enjoy hearing others talk. But if you learn the keys to receiving messages and make a strong effort to use them with your players, you'll be surprised by what you've been missing.

Pay Attention

First, you must pay attention and listen to what others have to communicate to you. That's not always easy when you're busy coaching and have many things competing for your attention. But in one-on-one or team meetings with players, you must focus on what they are telling you, both verbally and nonverbally. You'll be amazed at the little signals you pick up. Not only will this focused attention help you catch every word your players say, but you'll also notice your players' moods and physical states. In addition, you'll get an idea of your players' feelings toward you and other players on the team.

Listen Carefully

How you receive messages from others, perhaps more than anything else you do, demonstrates how much you care for the sender and what that person has to tell you. If you care little for your players or have little regard for what they have to say, it will show in how you attend and listen to them. You need to check yourself. Do you find your mind wandering to what you are going to do after practice while one of your players is talking to you? Do you frequently have to ask your players, "What did you say?" If so, you need to work on your receiving mechanics of attending and listening. But if you find that you're missing the messages your players send, perhaps the most critical question you should ask yourself is this: Do I care?

Providing Feedback

So far, we've discussed separately the sending and receiving of messages. But we all know that senders and receivers switch roles several times during an interaction. One person initiates a communication by sending a message to another person, who then receives the message. The receiver then becomes the sender by responding to the person who sent the initial message. These verbal and nonverbal responses are called *feedback*.

Your players will look to you for feedback all the time. They will want to know how you think they are performing, what you think of their ideas, and whether their efforts please you. You can respond in many different ways, and how you respond will strongly affect your players. They will react most favorably to positive feedback.

Praising players when they have performed or behaved well is an effective way of getting them to repeat (or try to repeat) that behavior. And positive feedback for effort is an especially effective way to motivate youngsters to work on difficult skills. So rather than shouting at and providing negative feedback to players who have made mistakes, you should try offering positive feedback and letting them know what they did correctly and how they can improve. Sometimes just the way you word feedback can make it more positive than negative. For example, instead of saying, "Don't hold the bat this way," you might say, "Grip the bat this way." Then your players will be focusing on what to do instead of what not to do.

Positive feedback can be verbal or nonverbal. Telling young players, especially in front of teammates, that they have performed well is a great way to boost their confidence. And a pat on the back or a high five communicates that you recognize a player's performance.

COACHING TIP Instead of just bringing out the gear, doing some stretching and throwing, and then going right into the day's practice, you should sit your players down and go over the last game or the last practice session. Ask them to grade their performance and to tell you what they think they need more practice in. Even young Babe Ruth Leaguers have a keen sense of how they did. Make them feel that they have a role in their improvement.

Communicating With Other Groups

In addition to sending and receiving messages and providing proper feedback to players, coaching also involves interacting with members of the coaching staff, parents, fans, umpires, and opposing coaches. If you don't communicate effectively with these groups, your coaching career will be unpleasant and short lived. So, try the following suggestions for communicating with these groups.

Coaching Staff

Before you hold your first practice, the coaching staff should meet and discuss the roles and responsibilities that each coach will undertake during the year. Depending on the number of assistant coaches, the staff responsibilities can be divided into different areas. For example, one coach may be in charge of the infielders, while another is responsible for overseeing batting practice. The head coach has the final responsibility for all phases of the game, but as much as possible, the assistant coaches should be responsible for their areas.

Before practices start, the coaching staff must also discuss and agree on terminology, plans for practice, game day organization, the method of communicating during practice and games, and game conditions. The coaches on your staff must present a united front and speak with one voice, and they must all take a similar approach to coaching, interaction with the players and parents, and interaction with one another. Disagreements should be discussed away from the field, and each coach should have a say as the staff comes to an agreement.

COACHING TIP Your coaching staff must be organized before practices and games. Work with your staff to ensure that tasks are completed by assigning specific tasks to each staff member. This will allow you to use time more efficiently, so you can focus on the actual practice or game.

Parents

A player's parents need to be assured that their child is under the direction of a coach who is both knowledgeable about the sport and concerned about the youngster's well-being. You can put their worries to rest by holding a preseason parent-orientation meeting in which you describe your background and your approach to coaching (see Preseason Meeting Topics). If parents contact you with a concern during the season, you should listen to them closely and try to offer positive responses. If you need to communicate with parents, you can catch them after a practice, give them a phone call, or send a text or e-mail. Messages sent to parents through players are too often lost, misinterpreted, or forgotten.

COACHING TIP Be clear about your expectations with parents. Every parent will lobby for more playing time for his or her own child—it's human nature. Make it clear that you will be glad to talk with parents about any aspect of their child's development as a person and as a ballplayer, but that playing time is a decision made by you and your coaches, and that this is something you won't discuss. Bringing this up early helps stave off misunderstandings and miscommunication later.

Preseason Meeting Topics

Before the Babe Ruth local league season starts, it is a good idea to have a meeting with the parents of your players. When parents are involved from the get-go, channels of communication and expectations are established before any issues arise. Listed below is a guideline of topics for your preseason parents' meeting.

1. Talk about yourself as an athlete, coach, or parent. Explain your coaching philosophy. Have the parents introduce themselves and include who their player is.
2. Outline the paperwork that is needed:
   • Emergency information: Collect vital information from parents by having them provide emergency information and consent for treatment for injury or illness (see the sample Emergency Information and Consent for Treatment Form at the end of this chapter). If any parent

has a medical concern regarding their child, discuss such in a private conversation, perhaps after the meeting.

- Informed Consent Form (see a sample at the end of this chapter): This form provides permission to participate in baseball and acknowledges that parents and players understand the inherent risks of playing the sport.

3. Go over the inherent risks of baseball and any other safety issues.

4. Discuss rules and expectations:
   - Team values: Explain the core values for your team.
   - Expectations of athletes: Explain the expectations you, as a coach, hold for your players.
   - Expectations of coaches: Explain the expectations you want your players and their parents to hold for you and your coaching staff.
   - Standard of conduct for coaches, players, and parents: Explain the policies for your team, for example, late policies, unsportsmanlike conduct policies, and practice and game policies.

5. Explain goals for the season:
   - Your goals as a coach for your team and players.
   - Parents' goals for their players.

6. Cover logistics:
   - Schedules: Hand out schedules to each parent. Review the season practice schedule, including the date, location, and time of each practice session.
   - Contact list: If available, hand out contact information to each parent.
   - Methods of communication: e-mail list, emergency telephone numbers, website.

7. Review the proper gear and attire that should be worn at practices and games. Inform parents of the date and time that uniforms and equipment will be handed out.

8. Discuss nutrition, hydration, and rest for players.

9. Discuss ways that parents can help with the team:
   - Provide snacks after games.
   - Be a scorekeeper for games.
   - Serve as a "Team Mom" or "Team Dad" to promote open communications between coaches, parents, and players.
   - Discuss any other volunteer positions that need to be filled.

10. End the meeting:
    - Provide time for questions and answers.
    - Thank them for their time.
    - Let them know you are excited for the season to start.

Fans

The stands probably won't be overflowing at your games, which means that you'll more easily hear the few fans who criticize your coaching. When you hear something negative about the job you're doing, don't respond. Keep calm, consider whether the message had any value, and, if not, forget it. Acknowledging critical, unwarranted comments from a fan during a game will only encourage others to voice their opinions. So, put away your "rabbit ears" and communicate to fans, through your actions, that you are a confident, competent coach. You must also prepare your players for fans' criticisms. Tell your players that it is you—not the spectators—that they should listen to. If you notice that one of your players is rattled by a fan's comment, you should reassure the player that your evaluation is more objective and favorable—and the one that counts.

Umpires

How you communicate with umpires will have a great influence on the way your players behave toward them. Therefore, you must set a good example. Greet umpires with a handshake, an introduction, and perhaps casual conversation about the upcoming game. Indicate your respect for them before, during, and after the game. Don't shout, make nasty remarks, or use disrespectful body gestures. Your players will see you do it, and they'll get the idea that such behavior is appropriate. Plus, if the umpire hears or sees you, the communication between the two of you will break down.

Opposing Coaches

Make an effort to visit with the coach of the opposing team before the game. During the game, don't get into a personal feud with the opposing coach. Remember, it's the kids, not the coaches, who are competing. And by getting along well with the opposing coach, you'll show your players that competition involves cooperation and sportsmanship.

Emergency Information and Consent for Treatment Form

Each player must complete and have signed.

Name of player: _____

Player's age:_____ Player's date of birth: _____

Home address: _____ City: _____

State: _____ Phone: _____

Contact Information

Parent's or guardian's name: _____

Address: _____

Daytime phone: _____Home phone: _____

Mobile phone: _____

Additional contact's name: _____

Relationship to player: _____

Address: _____

Daytime phone: _____Home phone: _____

Mobile phone: _____

Medical Information

Family physician:_____Phone: _____

List of any allergies: _____

Required medication: _____

_____

Any additional information we should know about your child's health or physical condition?_____

_____

Insurance Information

Name of league: _____

League accident insurance company (coach to fill in):_____

League accident insurance policy # (coach to fill in):_____

Parent's/guardian's health insurance company: _____

Parent's/guardian's health insurance policy #:_____

In case of an accident or illness, I hereby authorize a representative of Babe Ruth League, Inc. to use his/her judgment in obtaining immediate medical care.

DATE: _____SIGNED:_____

By: Parent or Guardian if Athlete is under the age of 18 **By:** Athlete if 18 or over

(Parents/guardians will be notified in case of serious illness or injury as quickly as they can be reached, but this will make immediate treatment possible.)

Informed Consent Form

I hereby give my permission for _____ to participate in _____ during the athletic season beginning on _____.

My child and I are aware that participating in _____ is a potentially hazardous activity. We assume all risks associated with participation in this sport, including but not limited to falls, contact with other participants, and the effects of the weather, traffic, and other reasonable-risk conditions associated with the sport. All such risks to my child are known and appreciated by my child and me.

We understand this informed consent form and agree to its conditions.

Player's signature: _____ Date: _____

Parent's or guardian's signature: _____ Date: _____

From Babe Ruth League, *Coaching Youth Baseball* (Champaign, IL: Human Kinetics, 2019). Adapted by permission from M. Flegel, *Sport First Aid*, 5th ed. (Champaign, IL: Human Kinetics, 2014), 15.

Understanding Rules and Equipment

3

Baseball is a complicated game played by two teams on a rather large field, with the players designated by positions. The game is governed by a thick rule book steeped in tradition. This introduction to the basic rules of baseball won't cover every rule of the game but instead will give you what you need to work with 4- to 18-year-old players. In this chapter, we cover specifics about some of the basics of the game, such as the number of players, field size, and field markings, depending on your team's age group. We also describe specifics such as equipment, player positions, game procedures, and rules. We wrap things up by describing officiating and identifying some of the most common officiating signals used by umpires.

Age Modifications for Baseball

Before we begin, let's consider some of the modifications that can be made to accommodate different age groups. Things such as the size of the field and the duration of the game can be adjusted for the various Babe Ruth League age groups to help accommodate player development and skill level. Suggested adjustments for Babe Ruth Baseball are as follows. These may vary depending on your league.

	Cal Ripken Minor Divisions 4- to 10-year-old players	Cal Ripken Major Division 11- to 12-year-old players	Babe Ruth 13-15 Division and Babe Ruth 16-18 Division
Players on the field per team	9	9	9
Players on team	15	15	15 players (13-15 Division); 18 players (16-18 Division)
Base paths	60 feet	60 or 70 feet	90 feet
Pitching distance	46 feet	46 or 50 feet	60 feet 6 inches
Fence (down the lines)	200 feet	225 feet	320 feet
Fence (to center field)	225 feet	275 feet	385 feet
Ball	Safety or softer ball is suggested for 4- to 7-year-old players Regulation ball (9.0 to 9.25 in. circumference; 5.0 to 5.25 oz. weight)	Regulation ball (9.0 to 9.25 in. circumference; 5.0 to 5.25 oz. weight)	Regulation ball (9.0 to 9.25 in. circumference; 5.0 to 5.25 oz. weight)

	Cal Ripken Minor Divisions 4- to 10-year-old players	Cal Ripken Major Division 11- to 12-year-old players	Babe Ruth 13-15 Division and Babe Ruth 16-18 Division
Bat	2 5/8 in. max barrel with USABat marking (NO BBCOR bats) T-ball bats with USABat T-ball stamp	2 5/8 in. max barrel with USABat marking (NO BBCOR bats)	2 5/8 in. max barrel with USABat marking or BBCOR .50 bats (13-15 Division) 2 5/8 in. max barrel, BBCOR .50 and no greater than −3 (16-18 Division)
Pitcher	Coach, machine, or player	Player	Player
Pitching restrictions	Pitcher may pitch 6 innings per calendar week. Pitcher must have two calendar days of rest between pitching assignments if he pitches in more than two innings in any one game. May elect to use a pitch count. For more information visit www.baberuthleague.org.	Pitcher may pitch 6 innings per calendar week. Pitcher must have two calendar days of rest between pitching assignments if he pitches in more than two innings in any one game. May elect to use a pitch count. For more information visit www.baberuthleague.org.	Pitcher may pitch 7 innings per calendar week. Pitcher must have two calendar days of rest between pitching assignments if he pitches in more than three innings in any one game. May elect to use a pitch count. For more information visit www.baberuthleague.org.
Innings	6	6	7
10-run rule	Game can be terminated once becoming regulation if one team is ahead by 10 or more runs and both teams have had equal times at bat or the home team is leading.	Game can be terminated once becoming regulation if one team is ahead by 10 or more runs and both teams have had equal times at bat or the home team is leading.	Game can be terminated once becoming regulation if one team is ahead by 10 or more runs and both teams have had equal times at bat or the home team is leading.
Lead-offs	No	Yes (50/70 program)	Yes
Steals	Yes	Yes	Yes
Extra player (EP)	May elect to add a tenth player to the batting order. The EP will be treated as any other starter.	May elect to add a tenth player to the batting order. The EP will be treated as any other starter.	May elect to add a tenth player to the batting order. The EP will be treated as any other starter.

How the Game Is Played

Baseball is a challenging game played by two teams of nine players who alternate turns on offense and defense, with each team having a turn at bat every inning. The game is played on a diamond-shaped field with a base in each corner. The objective of the game is for the offense to hit the ball and score runs by running around the bases and safely advancing to home plate before the defense makes three outs each inning. Although the concept is simple, specific offensive and defensive aspects of the game are executed differently based on the level of play and the game situation. Additionally, the field that the game is played on may vary depending on the age level of your players and the facility where the game is played. Figure 3.1 shows the field markings for a standard baseball field.

Several areas of the field shown in figure 3.1 are referred to with special baseball terminology. Here are a few definitions:

- **Foul lines.** Lines that run from home to first base and from home to third base and extend beyond those bases to the outfield fence.
- **Fair territory.** The area inside the foul lines, including the lines; anything outside the lines is foul.
- **Infield.** Fair territory around the base portion of the field.

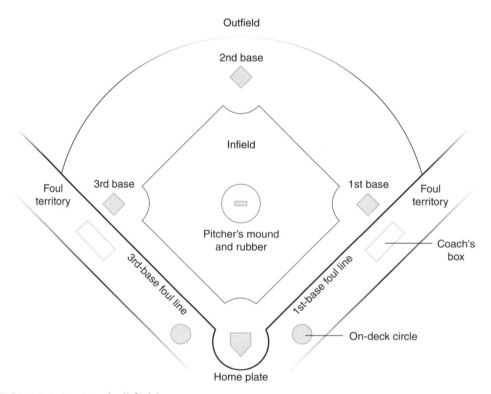

FIGURE 3.1   Baseball field areas.

- **Pitcher's rubber.** The plate on which the pitcher must begin pitching.
- **Pitcher's mound.** A circular area around the pitcher's rubber.
- **Batter's boxes.** Lines on either side of home plate that define the area in which the batter must stand.
- **Coach's boxes.** A lined area near first base and third base where the coaches position themselves during a game when their team is batting.
- **Outfield.** Fair territory in the grassy portion of the field beyond the infield.

Player Equipment

The standard pieces of equipment for baseball include bases, balls, bats, gloves, helmets, and other appropriate apparel. But how do you know when this equipment meets proper specifications and is in good repair? As a Babe Ruth League coach, you must examine the condition of each item you distribute to players. Also make sure that the pieces of equipment they furnish themselves meet acceptable standards. You should ensure that each player on your team is outfitted properly, and you may want to demonstrate to players how to properly wear their equipment. Following is additional information on the common equipment used in baseball:

Bases

Babe Ruth League, Inc. suggests your organization use breakaway bases. A breakaway base is different from a standard base in that it is manufactured in two pieces; the top piece dislodges when a player slides into it with force, significantly reducing ankle injuries. Although breakaway bases are usually more expensive, they are recommended for all age groups.

Balls

Regulation balls are used for ages 8 through 18 (as noted in Age Modifications for Baseball). Safety balls, which are softer, rubber-coated balls, are recommended for 4- to 7-year-old players. Using safety balls helps prevent players from developing a fear of hitting or catching a ball, which can impede their skill development.

Bats

The size of the bat should be appropriate to the player, and the handle of the bat should be thin enough that the player can easily grip it with both hands. Additionally, a bat with a large hitting end tapering down to a small handle gives the greatest sweet spot—that is, the greatest area with which to make solid hits. Check with your local Babe Ruth League president to make sure your bat is approved for use in your league.

Babe Ruth League, Inc. Bat Rules

- **Cal Ripken Division:** All non-wood bats must have the USABat marking and a maximum barrel size of 2 5/8 inches. No BBCOR bats are permitted in the Cal Ripken Division. For the T-ball division, bats must be marked with the USABat T-ball stamp.
- **Babe Ruth Baseball 13-15 Division:** All non-wood bats must have the USABat marking or be marked BBCOR .50 and have a maximum barrel size of 2 5/8 inches.
- **Babe Ruth Baseball 16-18 Division:** All non-wood bats MUST be a BBCOR .50 and no greater than -3 with a maximum barrel size of 2 5/8 inches.

Gloves

The size of a player's glove should also be appropriate to the player, and you will need to help your players select proper-fitting gloves. As a rule of thumb, it is better to start with a smaller glove, because an oversized glove will be difficult to control and can hinder skill development. Specialty gloves are also manufactured for catchers and first basemen. A catcher's mitt is padded and rounded so that the ball easily lands in the pocket. The extra padding also helps ensure the safety of the player using the glove. The first-base player's glove is similar to a catcher's mitt in that it has a large pocket, but it is longer and not as rounded. You will also want to teach your players how to break in, or condition, their gloves. Well-conditioned gloves will help improve the players' ability to hold onto the ball.

Helmets

Your players must wear helmets while batting and running the bases. An on-deck player (the player who will be hitting next) must also wear a helmet, as should players serving as base coaches and the bat boy or girl. Babe Ruth League recommends helmets certified by the National Operating Committee on Standards for Athletic Equipment (NOCSAE), with double flaps. Face masks on helmets are optional. Check to make sure your players' helmets fit correctly and are in good condition.

Apparel

Players should wear baseball shoes with rubber cleats (or metal spikes where allowed). Tying the laces of the shoes in a double knot can help keep them from coming untied, which can cause a player to trip. Players should wear caps to keep hair and sun out of their eyes; they should keep their hair tucked inside the cap to prevent it from obstructing vision. Players should not be allowed to wear jewelry, watches, or other metal objects during practice and games. (Medical alert bracelets or necklaces are not considered jewelry. If worn, they must be taped to the body.)

Special Equipment

The catcher will need a helmet that covers the entire head and provides throat protection, a chest protector, and shin guards. Knee savers are also available that help eliminate fatigue. You should also encourage all male players to wear a protective cup.

Player Positions

Baseball is played with nine players on the field on defense. Each defensive position is associated with a number, as shown in figure 3.2. The main defensive players are the pitcher and catcher, known as the battery. Infielders, who handle ground balls and pop-ups on the dirt portion of the field, include the first-base player, second-base player, shortstop, and third-base player. The outfielders are the right fielder, center fielder, and left fielder.

Babe Ruth Baseball (all divisions) has the Extra Player Rule, as described in Age Modifications for Baseball.

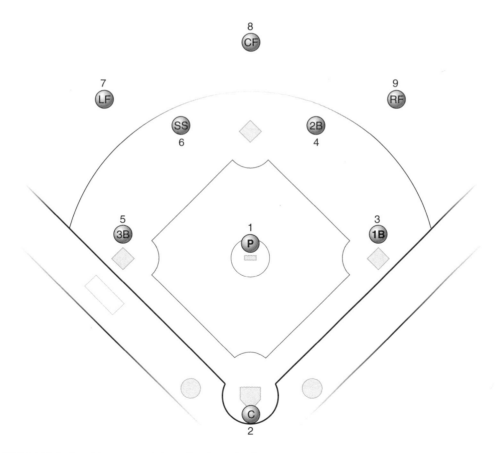

FIGURE 3.2   Player positions for baseball.

Young players should be given a chance to play a variety of positions. By playing different positions, they'll have a better all-around playing experience and may stay more interested in the sport. Furthermore, they'll gain a better understanding of the many technical and tactical skills used in the game. This will also help them appreciate the efforts of their teammates who play positions they find difficult. Following are descriptions of the positions in baseball, along with the number associated with each position. These descriptions will help you place your players in positions that best suit their individual strengths:

- **Pitcher (1).** Arm strength and control are indications that a player may make a successful pitcher. Your pitcher should also be a smart, tough, and confident competitor who will rise to the occasion when confronted with a challenge. A solid mental and emotional makeup will also help make a pitcher effective, because pitchers must stay poised throughout the game.

- **Catcher (2).** The catcher is considered the quarterback in baseball because all action takes place in front of this player. Good catchers are rugged individuals, and if they are not big and strong, then they must be tough. The position requires strength, endurance, and great hand–eye coordination. The catcher is up and down from a squat position on every pitch, throwing balls back to the pitcher or infielders, backing up first base on ground balls when other runners aren't on base, and chasing short foul balls.

- **First base (3).** The first-base player makes more unusual plays than any other position. The ability to catch all types of thrown balls is essential for a first-base player. Above-average height, speed, grace of movement, good fielding of ground balls, and good judgment of infield flies are other qualities of a good first-base player. A strong and accurate arm is a bonus at this position.

- **Second base (4).** Players of all different statures have become excellent at playing the second-base position. Whether big or little, however, a second-base player must have a sure pair of hands to field ground balls, pop flies, and thrown balls. Moreover, a second-base player must be able to foresee fielding situations and react in an instant.

- **Third base (5).** The third-base player must possess agility, good hands, and quick reflexes. This player must be able to come in fast on the ball and throw accurately while running at top speed. The third-base player must be able to make off-balance throws and bare-handed pickups on bunts and slowly hit balls. The third-base player must also have a strong arm to make the long throws to first base.

- **Shortstop (6).** The shortstop will be required to make more tough plays than any other player on the field. A shortstop must be alert, be able to start and stop quickly, possess a sure pair of hands, and have a strong throwing arm. This player must also have quick reactions.

- **Left field (7).** The left fielder can have less speed and a weaker arm than any other outfielder because many of the throws made from this position do not cover a great distance. However, this player must still be alert, have a good arm to the plate, and be a good fielder of ground balls. The left fielder backs up third base whenever necessary.

- **Center field (8).** The center fielder covers more territory than any other player and will make the greatest percentage of outfield put-outs. This player usually has the best speed of the outfielders and must have a strong arm. The center fielder backs up at second base on all sacrifice bunts and every attempted put-out at second.

- **Right field (9).** The right fielder, above all else, must have a strong, accurate throwing arm. This player is responsible for backing up first base on all bunted balls, all throws from the catcher to first base, and all plays when there is a possibility that the ball will come into right field, such as on a wild throw. The right fielder also backs up at second base on all balls hit to the left side of the diamond.

Rules of Play

Baseball rules are designed to make the game run smoothly and safely and to prevent either team from gaining an unfair advantage. Throw out the rules and a baseball game can quickly turn chaotic. All Babe Ruth Baseball games must be played in accordance with the official baseball playing rules. The only exceptions are those listed in the Babe Ruth League, Inc. baseball rules and regulations. Following is an overview of some of the basic rules in baseball.

Batting and the Batting Order

The home team will bat second, after the visiting team, and is generally the team whose field is being used. In leagues where all teams use the same fields, the home team is predetermined by league officials. If the home team has not been determined, such as in tournament play, a coin toss is usually used by the umpire-in-chief to determine the home team.

The coach of each team must submit a batting order to the umpire-in-chief before the start of a game (this takes place at a pregame conference involving the coaches and umpires). Other copies of the batting order are usually given to the scorekeeper and the opposing coach. The batting order must list the full names of the players starting at each position in the lineup as well as each player's uniform number. This batting order must be followed throughout the game. It should also list the names of available substitutes (when substitutions are made, the substitute must occupy the same spot in the batting order that the original player occupied—see Substitutions for more information). Additionally, for younger age groups, it is highly recommended that all players on the roster have a turn at bat whether or not they are playing in the field.

Scoring

A run is scored if an offensive player touches first, second, and third bases and home plate in order without being called out. The batter may be called out in several ways: a strikeout (when three strikes are called on the hitter); a ground-out (when the batted ball touches the ground before being caught by a fielder and is thrown to the first-base player, whose foot must touch the base before the batter arrives); or a fly-out (when the batted ball is caught by a fielder before it touches the ground). A runner may also be called out on a tag-out (when the runner is tagged by an opponent who is in possession of the ball) or a force-out (when an opponent who is in possession of the ball touches a base before the runner arrives, and the runner cannot retreat to the previous base because a teammate is already advancing there). In rare circumstances, players may also be called out for interfering with a player or touching a live ball. In leagues where stealing is not allowed, players may be called out for leaving the base too early.

The team with the most runs at the end of the game is the winner. Extra innings are played to determine the winner if a game is tied at the end of regulation play. Only runs that are scored before the third out of each inning will count. For example, if a player scores a run, but a trailing player is forced out at a base for the third out, the run will not count.

Using a Scorebook

Who needs instant replay? A well-kept scorebook can tell you what happened on every play of the game—where the batter ended up, how far other runners advanced, and how the out was made. Your league may have provided you with a scorebook when you signed on to coach; if not, be sure to purchase one. Most coaches keep score for both teams, so they can look back later in the season to see how a team performed before playing that team again. You may prefer to keep the game score yourself so you can make notes during the game, or you can ask an assistant coach or a parent to keep score if you prefer to focus on the game. For leagues that don't have scoreboards or official scorekeepers, the home team is responsible for keeping the official scorebook for the game.

Using a scorebook is easy once you know the numbering system (as shown in figure 3.2 and discussed previously in Player Positions) and a few abbreviations:

1B: one-base hit
2B: two-base hit
3B: three-base hit
BB: base on balls; walk
BK: balk
DP: double play
E: error (also indicates the fielder making the error, for example, E5)
F: fly-out
FC: fielder's choice
FF: foul fly
HP: hit by pitch

HR: home run

IW: intentional walk

K: strikeout (swinging)

Kc: strikeout (called)

L: line drive

OS: out stealing

PB: passed ball

RBI: run batted in (also list the batting order number of the player credited with the RBI)

SAC: sacrifice (can be used for bunt or hit)

SB: stolen base

TP: triple play

WP: wild pitch

Every time a batter goes to the plate, the scorekeeper will use the position numbers to indicate how the player reached the base or how the player was retired. For example, figure 3.3 shows a sample scorebook for the following seven batters.

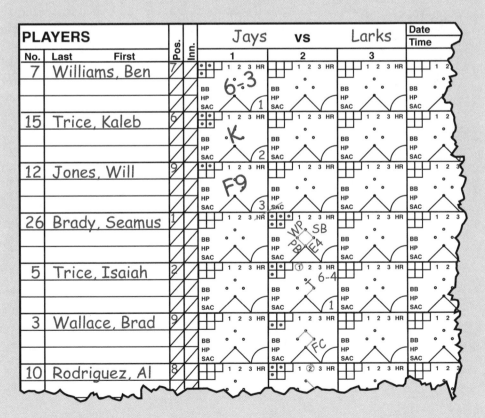

FIGURE 3.3 Sample scorebook.

> continued

1. *Williams grounds out to the shortstop on the 2-1 pitch.* Write 6-3 across the middle of the diamond in the box. Put a number 1 in the arced space in the corner to indicate it was the first out. Keep track of subsequent outs the same way.

2. *K. Trice, the next batter, strikes out on the fifth pitch.* Write K across the middle of the box.

3. *The third batter, Jones, flies out to the right fielder, ending the first inning.* Use F9. (F stands for a fly-out. If the ball had been hit harder, you could have used an L, for line drive.) Finally, draw a diagonal line across the lower right corner of the box to indicate the last batter in the inning. This will allow you to quickly see who is up to bat first in the next inning.

4. *On a 3-2 pitch, Brady hits a ground ball to the second-base player, who makes an error that allows him to be safe at first.* Darken the line between home and first to indicate Brady's movement. Write E4 under the line to show how he got to first base.

5. *On the first pitch to I. Trice, Brady steals second base.* Show this by darkening the line in Brady's box between first and second base in the diamond and placing an SB (for stolen base) above the line.

6. *The next pitch to the batter goes over the catcher's head to the backstop, allowing Brady to advance to third.* Darken the line in Brady's box between second and third base to indicate Brady's movement. Write WP over the line to indicate that he got to third on a wild pitch.

7. *The very next pitch goes through the catcher's legs, and Brady scores a run.* Darken the line in Brady's box between third base and home on the diamond. Write PB (for passed ball) under the line. Some scorers will also fill in the interior space of the diamond to make it easier to spot runs quickly when viewing the scorebook.

8. *Finally, I. Trice, hits the next pitch into the outfield for a single.* Darken the line from home to first, then circle the 1 in the top of the box to indicate a single.

9. *The next batter, Wallace, hits a ground ball to the shortstop, who throws to second base for a force-out.* Wallace is safe at first on a fielder's choice. Darken the line from home to first for Wallace because he is safe at first base. Write FC below the line to indicate how he got there. Also, in Trice's box, draw a line along the diamond halfway to second base and then draw a perpendicular line across the end of this line. This signifies that Trice was out. Write 6-4 to show how the out was made and also put a number 1 in the arced space in the corner.

10. *Rodriguez, the next batter, hits a double.* Continue in the same way as above, circling the 2 in the top of the box. Also, darken the lines in Wallace's box to indicate how far he advanced.

Baseball No-Nos

It's inevitable that your players will violate minor rules during practices and games. But you must make it clear to your players that some actions are unacceptable on the baseball field and can result in an out or an ejection, depending on the severity of the infraction. Here are some examples:

- Throwing the bat, either wildly after hitting the ball or intentionally in frustration for being out
- Intentionally trying to interfere with a defensive player while running the bases
- Intentionally running into a defensive player covering the base rather than sliding or slowing down to avoid a collision
- Swearing, taunting an opponent, or arguing with the umpire

Your role as a Babe Ruth League coach is not limited to teaching fundamentals; you must also promote good sporting behavior both on and off the field. For example, encourage your infielders to help a runner up after a slide into the base once the ball has been called dead. Encourage your defense to leave the ball in the pitcher's circle at the end of the inning so it's there for the other team. Instruct your team to retrieve any balls your offense hits outside the fences and to return them to the umpire. Both your opponents and the umpire will appreciate this behavior.

Substitutions

Per the Babe Ruth League's re-entry rule, any of the starting players may withdraw and re-enter the game once, provided such player occupies the same batting position wherever he is in the line-up. A substitute who is withdrawn may not re-enter. All pitchers are governed by the provisions of Official Babe Ruth Baseball Rule 3.05 if withdrawn while on the mound pitching. A pitcher withdrawn while a batter or base runner may re-enter the game immediately. If the pitcher is removed from the game because of a second trip in the same inning, he may re-enter the game in any position with the exception of pitcher.

Babe Ruth League, Inc. will allow re-entry of already used players if all substitutes have been used and injury occurs, or a player is ejected. Selection of the substitute must be made by the opposing manager. The injured or ejected player, once removed from the game, cannot re-enter.

Umpires

Umpires are officials who enforce the rules of the game. At the youth level, there are usually two umpires overseeing the game—one at home plate (the plate

umpire) and another positioned in or near the infield according to the game situation (the base umpire). If no one is on base, the base umpire stands in the outfield near the first-base line so that he or she is in position to call plays at first base. When first base or first and second are occupied, the base umpire moves to the inside of the infield to be better able to call plays at first or second. Plays at third base and home are usually called by the plate umpire. In circumstances where an umpire is taken out of position during the course of a play, there is a pre-determined rotation system that umpires should learn and use. It is recommended that all umpires be certified by the National Umpire Association of Babe Ruth League.

See figure 3.4 for common officiating signals used by umpires.

FIGURE 3.4 Some signals commonly used by umpires are *(a)* time-out, *(b)* strike, *(c)* out, *(d)* safe, *(e)* foul, and *(f)* fair.

Challenging Calls

Umpires decide whether a pitch is a ball or a strike, a hit is fair or foul, and a runner is safe or out. The home plate umpire is the ultimate decision maker on any ruling, and you and your players are not allowed to appeal judgment calls (e.g., ball or strike, safe or out, fair or foul). You can appeal rule interpretations, such as whether a runner missed a base or left a base early on a caught fly ball (i.e., didn't tag up) or whether a batter swung at a pitch or checked his swing. All appeals should be made calmly and professionally, without raising your voice or questioning an umpire's skills. Here are a couple of examples of the proper way to appeal a play:

- A batter may start to swing the bat and then change his mind and stop, or "check," the swing. If the umpire calls a ball, the catcher may appeal the call to the base umpire for a decision on whether the batter checked his swing in time or if he rolled his wrists, brought the bat out in front of the body, or made an attempt to hit the pitch before checking the swing.

- A fielder or coach may appeal if he thinks a runner left a base too early when tagging up or missed touching a base when running. If the ball is dead (that is, the ball has been returned to the pitcher and time has been called), an infielder or coach can appeal to the umpire, asking if the runner left early or missed the base. If the umpire decides he did, that runner is declared out. If the ball is still live (that is, a fielder is still in possession of the ball and hasn't returned it to the pitcher), the fielder can appeal by touching the base that was missed or left too soon, and the umpire will make the call.

There may also be situations where you as a coach will want to challenge a call based on a rule interpretation or your opinion that an umpire couldn't see a play. For example, in order for a force-out to be called, the base player must have control of the ball. Let's say your baserunner is called out at first on a force play, but the first-base player was bobbling the throw when your runner reached the base. The base umpire was out of position and didn't have a good angle to see the bobbled catch, so you may respectfully approach the umpire and make an appeal, asking, "Did you see if the first-base player had control of the ball on that play?" If the base umpire didn't see that part of the play and wants help, he or she may ask the plate umpire to help with the ruling. The coach is the only person who may make an appeal of this kind.

Appeals must be made before the next pitch or, if at the end of the inning, before all infielders have left fair territory. On a game-ending play, the appeal must be made before the umpires leave the field. Once an umpire has responded to your appeal with a decision, it is over, and you can't continue to appeal. If you continue to protest, raise your voice, or use inappropriate language, you may be given a warning or even ejected from the game. Interrupting the game to argue with an umpire won't change the call, and it sets a poor example for your players. Keep in mind that appeals have a place only in higher levels of play with older players. However, at all levels, you should immediately consult with the umpires if at any time you feel that the officiating jeopardizes the safety of your players.

One of your players rounds third and heads for home plate. The throw from the outfield arrives at home just ahead of the runner. Sliding to avoid the tag, your player catches a leg on one of the catcher's shin guards. The runner is called safe by the umpire, but he is not getting up and seems to be in pain. What do you do?

No coach wants to see players get hurt. But injury remains a reality of sport participation; consequently, you must be prepared to provide first aid when injuries occur. Fortunately, coaches can institute many preventive measures to reduce risk. In this chapter, we describe steps you can take to prevent injuries, first aid and emergency responses for when injuries occur, and your legal responsibilities as a coach. The safety, protection, and well-being of our young players is always Babe Ruth League's top priority.

Game Plan for Safety

Babe Ruth League has implemented many safety innovations over the years to ensure participants are provided with a safe, healthy, and educational environment in which to enjoy the game of baseball. While you can't prevent all injuries from happening, you can take preventive measures that give your players the best possible chance for injury-free participation. To help you create the safest possible environment for your players, we'll explore what you can do in these areas:

- Preseason physical examination
- Physical conditioning
- Facilities and equipment inspection
- Player matchups and inherent risks
- Proper supervision and record keeping
- Environmental conditions

Preseason Physical Examination

We recommend that your players have a physical examination before participating in baseball. The exam should address the most likely areas of medical concern and identify youngsters at high risk. We also suggest that you have the players' parents or guardians sign a participation agreement form (this will be discussed in more detail later in this chapter) and a consent for treatment form to allow their children to be treated in case of an emergency. For sample forms that cover both of these areas, please see the Informed Consent and Emergency Information and Consent for Treatment forms at the end of chapter 2.

Physical Conditioning

Players need to be in shape (or get in shape) to play the game at the level expected. They must have adequate cardiorespiratory fitness and muscular fitness.

Cardiorespiratory fitness involves the body's ability to use oxygen and fuels efficiently to power muscle contractions. As players get in better shape, their bodies are able to more efficiently deliver oxygen to fuel muscles and carry off carbon dioxide and other wastes. At times, baseball will require lots of running and exertion. Youngsters who aren't as fit as their peers often overextend in trying to keep up, which can result in light-headedness, nausea, fatigue, and potential injury.

Try to remember that the players' goals are to participate, learn, and have fun. Therefore, you must keep the players active, attentive, and involved with every phase of practice. If you do, they will attain higher levels of cardiorespiratory fitness as the season progresses simply by taking part in practice. However, you should watch closely for signs of low cardiorespiratory fitness; don't let your players do too much until they're fit. You might privately counsel youngsters who appear overly winded, suggesting that they train outside of practice (under proper supervision) to increase their fitness.

Muscular fitness encompasses strength, muscular endurance, power, speed, and flexibility. This type of fitness is affected by physical maturity, as well as strength training and other types of training. Your players will likely exhibit a relatively wide range of muscular fitness. Those who have greater muscular fitness will be able to run faster and throw harder. They will also sustain fewer muscular injuries, and any injuries that do occur will tend to be minor. And in case of injury, recovery is faster in those with higher levels of muscular fitness.

Two other components of fitness and injury prevention are the warm-up and the cool-down. Although young bodies are generally very limber, they can become tight through inactivity. The warm-up should address each muscle group and should elevate the heart rate in preparation for strenuous activity. Players should warm up for 5 to 10 minutes using a combination of light running, jumping, and stretching. As practice winds down, slow players' heart rates with an easy jog or walk. Then have the players stretch for 5 minutes to help prevent tight muscles before the next practice or game.

COACHING TIP   Younger players may not be aware of when they need a break for water and a short rest; therefore, you need to work breaks into your practice schedules. It is a good idea to have water available at all times during the practice session. This will eliminate the need for long water breaks during practice.

Facilities and Equipment Inspection

Over the years, Babe Ruth League has been proud to provide our leagues with valuable input and services to help them provide a safe environment for everyone at youth baseball games.

Facilities

Another way to prevent injuries is to regularly inspect the field on which your players practice and play. Remove hazards, report conditions you cannot remedy, and request maintenance as necessary. If unsafe conditions exist, you should either make adaptations to prevent risk to your players' safety or stop the practice or game until safe conditions have been restored. Refer to the Facilities and Equipment Checklist at the end of this chapter to help guide you in verifying that facilities and equipment are safe. Note that installation of all equipment must meet manufacturers' requirements.

Equipment

You can also prevent injuries by checking the quality and fit of uniforms, practice attire, and any protective equipment used by your players. Make sure the players' equipment fits properly and is not worn out. A helmet that is too large can cover a batter's eyes and prevent him or her from reacting to an inside pitch. A helmet that is too small might not provide proper protection. Catcher's gear that is too large might shift and leave an area of the body exposed. If the gear is too small, it might not cover all the body parts that it should. Other equipment guidelines to consider:

- **Bats:** Use appropriate bats based on the following information detailing approved bats for Babe Ruth League:
  » **Cal Ripken Division:** All non-wood bats must have the USABat marking and a maximum barrel size of 2 5/8 inches. No BBCOR bats are permitted in the Cal Ripken Division. For the T-ball division, bats must be marked with the USABat T-ball stamp.
  » **Babe Ruth Baseball 13-15 Division:** All non-wood bats must have the USABat marking or be marked BBCOR .50 with a maximum barrel size of 2 5/8 inches.
  » **Babe Ruth Baseball 16-18 Division:** All non-wood bats MUST be a BBCOR .50 and no greater than -3 with a maximum barrel size of 2 5/8 inches.
- **Protective headgear:** During practice and all games, players shall wear a batting helmet on deck, at bat, while a base runner, and while in the coach's box. The batting helmet must cover the top of the head, have extended earflaps that cover both ears, and properly fit the player wearing it. The batting helmet shall not have a chrome or mirror-like surface, which is distracting and may be dangerous to other players.

- **Ball and bat boys and girls:** During local league and tournament play, ball and bat boys and girls must wear helmets while out of the dugout.

- **Catcher's mask, helmet, and throat protector (all divisions, except Cal Ripken Division):** Any player, manager, or coach warming up a pitcher at any location shall wear a mask. An extended dangling throat protector is considered a required part of the catcher's mask. Hockey-style catcher's masks with built-in extended throat protection are approved and do not require an extended dangling throat protector. The catcher's mask shall not have a chrome or mirror-like surface.

- **Catcher's mask, helmet, throat protector, and protective cup (Cal Ripken Division):** The catcher's helmet must cover the ears. Hockey-style catcher's masks are approved as meeting this requirement.

- **Shoes (Cal Ripken Division):** Shoes with metal cleats or spikes are not permitted to be worn by any player, coach, or manager.

- **Jewelry:** Jewelry is prohibited. Players shall not wear jewelry. Medical alert and religious bracelets or necklaces are not considered jewelry. If worn, they must be taped to the body.

- **Protective cup:** No baseball player should step on a field without wearing a protective cup. The earlier a player gets used to wearing a cup, the easier it will be for him to wear it consistently.

Player Matchups and Inherent Risks

If possible, Babe Ruth League, Inc. recommends that you group players in two-year age increments for the younger age divisions. You'll encounter fewer mismatches in physical maturation with narrow age ranges. Even so, two 12-year-old boys might differ by 90 pounds in weight, a foot in height, and 3 or 4 years in emotional and intellectual maturity. This presents dangers for the less mature. If this occurs, and whenever possible, you should match players against opponents of similar size and physical maturity. Such an approach gives smaller, less mature youngsters a better chance to succeed and avoid injury while providing more mature players with a greater challenge. Closely supervise games so that the more mature players do not put the less mature at undue risk.

Although proper matching helps protect you from certain liability concerns, you must also warn players of the inherent risks involved in playing baseball, because "failure to warn" is one of the most successful arguments in lawsuits against coaches. So, thoroughly explain the inherent risks of baseball, and make sure each player knows, understands, and appreciates those risks. You can learn more about these inherent risks by talking with your Babe Ruth League administrators.

The preseason parent-orientation meeting is a good opportunity to explain the risks of the sport to both parents and players. It is also a good time to have both the players and their parents sign a participation agreement form or waiver releasing you from liability should an injury occur. You should work with your league when creating these forms or waivers, and the forms should be reviewed by legal counsel before presentation. These forms or waivers do not relieve you of responsibility for your players' well-being, but they are recommended by lawyers and may help you in the event of a lawsuit.

> **COACHING TIP** If your players vary largely in size and the bigger players tend to take over drills, you should design drills and games so that those players are less dominant. For example, in a hitting game, you can force the bigger players to bat from their weak side (e.g., if the player is a left-handed hitter, make him hit right-handed). This may prevent bigger players from overpowering smaller players, and it has the added benefit of helping players develop switch-hitting skills.

Proper Supervision and Record Keeping

To ensure players' safety, you must provide both general supervision and specific supervision. *General supervision* means that you are in the area of activity so that you can see and hear what is happening. You should be

- on the field and in position to supervise the players even before the formal practice begins,
- immediately accessible to the activity and able to oversee the entire activity,
- alert to conditions that may be dangerous to players and ready to take action to protect players,
- able to react immediately and appropriately to emergencies, and
- present on the field until the last player has been picked up after the practice or game.

Specific supervision is the direct supervision of an activity at practice. For example, you should provide specific supervision when you teach new skills and should continue it until your players understand the requirements of the activity, the risks involved, and their own ability to perform in light of these risks. You must also provide specific supervision when you notice players breaking rules or a change in the condition of your players. As a general rule, the more dangerous the activity, the more specific the supervision required. This suggests that more specific supervision is required with younger and less experienced players.

As part of your supervision duty, you are expected to foresee potentially dangerous situations and to be positioned to help prevent them. This requires that you know baseball well, especially the rules that are intended to provide for safety. Prohibit dangerous horseplay, and hold training sessions only under safe weather conditions. These specific supervisory activities, applied consistently, will make the play environment safer for your players and will help protect you from liability if a mishap occurs.

For further protection, keep records of your season plans, practice plans, and players' injuries. Season and practice plans come in handy when you need evidence that players have been taught certain skills, whereas accurate, detailed injury report forms offer protection against unfounded lawsuits. Ask for these forms from your league board (see the end of this chapter for a sample Injury Report Form), and hold onto these records for several years so that an "old baseball injury" of a former player doesn't come back to haunt you.

COACHING TIP Supervision is very important to ensure that the baseball skills you teach are performed in a consistent manner. The more adults that can help supervise the skills, the better the players can learn and perform those skills.

Environmental Conditions

Most health problems caused by environmental factors are related to excessive heat or cold, although you should also consider other environmental factors such as severe weather and air pollution. A little thought about the potential problems and a little effort to ensure adequate protection for your players will prevent most serious emergencies related to environmental conditions.

COACHING TIP Encourage players to drink plenty of water before, during, and after practice. Water makes up 45 to 65 percent of a young-ster's body weight, and even a small amount of water loss can cause severe consequences in the body's systems. It doesn't have to be hot and humid for players to become dehydrated, nor is thirst an accurate indicator. In fact, by the time players are aware of their thirst, they are long overdue for a drink.

Heat

On hot, humid days the body has difficulty cooling itself. Because the air is already saturated with water vapor (humidity), sweat doesn't evaporate as easily. Therefore, body sweat is a less effective cooling agent, and the body retains extra heat. Hot, humid environments put players at risk of heat exhaustion and heat-stroke (see more on these in Serious Injuries later in the chapter). And if you think it's hot or humid, it's worse for the kids, not only because they're more active, but also because kids under the age of 12 have more difficulty regulating their body temperature than adults do. To provide for players' safety in hot or humid conditions, take the following preventive measures:

- Monitor weather conditions and adjust training sessions accordingly. Table 4.1 shows the specific air temperatures and humidity percentages that can be hazardous.

- Acclimatize players to exercising in high heat and humidity. Athletes can adjust to high heat and humidity in 7 to 10 days. During this period, hold practices at low to moderate activity levels and give the players fluid breaks every 20 minutes.

- Switch to light clothing. Players should wear shorts and white T-shirts.

- Identify and monitor players who are prone to heat illness. This would include players who are overweight, heavily muscled, or out of shape and players who work excessively hard or have suffered previous heat illness. Closely monitor these players and give them fluid breaks every 15 to 20 minutes.

- Make sure players replace fluids lost through sweat. Encourage players to drink 17 to 20 ounces of fluid 2 to 3 hours before each practice or game, to drink 7 to 10 ounces every 20 minutes during practice and after practice, and to drink 16 to 24 ounces of fluid for every pound lost. Fluids such as water and sports drinks are preferable during games and practices (suggested intakes are based on NATA [National Athletic Trainers' Association] recommendations).

- Encourage players to replenish electrolytes (e.g., sodium and potassium) that are lost through sweat. The best way to replace these nutrients—as well as others such as carbohydrate (energy) and protein (muscle building)—is by eating a balanced diet.

Sun

Getting too much sun can be risky. UVA and UVB rays can cause a bad sunburn and skin damage that leads to skin cancer. The sun is most dangerous between 10:00 a.m. and 4:00 p.m. Babe Ruth League suggests that you advise the parents of your players to bring and use sunscreen that is water and sweat resistant with an SPF of 30 or higher that has broad- or multi-spectrum protection for both UVA and UVB rays. Sunscreen should be applied 30 minutes before going outside and reapplied halfway through games, practices, or other activities. Apply

TABLE 4.1 Warm-Weather Precautions

Temperature (°F)	Humidity	Precautions
80-90	<70%	Monitor players prone to heat illness
80-90	>70%	5 min rest after 30 min of practice
90-100	<70%	5 min rest after 30 min of practice
90-100	>70%	Short practices in evenings or early mornings

it even on cloudy days, as 80% of the sun's ultraviolet rays can sneak through clouds on even the most overcast days.

Cold

When a person is exposed to cold weather, body temperature starts to drop below normal. To counteract this reaction, the body shivers to create heat and reduces blood flow to the extremities to conserve heat in the core of the body. But no matter how effective its natural heating mechanism is, the body will better withstand cold temperatures if it is prepared to handle them. To reduce the risk of cold-related illnesses, make sure players wear appropriate protective clothing, and keep the players active to maintain body heat. Also monitor the windchill factor because it can drastically affect the severity of players' responses to the weather. The windchill factor index is shown in figure 4.1.

Severe Weather

Severe weather refers to a host of potential dangers, including lightning storms, tornadoes, hail, and heavy rains. Lightning is of special concern because it can come up quickly and can cause great harm or even kill. For each 5-second count from the flash of lightning to the bang of thunder, lightning is one mile away. A flash–bang of 10 seconds means lightning is two miles away; a flash–bang of 15 seconds indicates lightning is three miles away. A practice or competition should be stopped if lightning is six miles away or closer (30 seconds or less from

Temperature (°F)

	0	5	10	15	20	25	30	35	40
Flesh may freeze within one minute									
40	-29	-22	-15	-8	-1	6	13	20	27
35	-27	-21	-14	-7	0	7	14	21	28
30	-26	-19	-12	-5	1	8	15	22	28
25	-24	-17	-11	-4	3	9	16	23	29
20	-22	-15	-9	-2	4	11	17	24	30
15	-19	-13	-7	0	6	13	19	25	32
10	-16	-10	-4	3	9	15	21	27	34
5	-11	-5	1	7	13	19	25	31	36

Wind speed (mph)

Windchill temperature (°F)

FIGURE 4.1 Windchill factor index.

Adapted from National Weather Service, "Wind Chill Chart," last modified November 1, 2001, https://www.weather.gov/safety/cold-wind-chill-chart.

flash to bang). In addition to these suggestions, your league, district, or state association may also have rules that you will want to consider in severe weather.

Babe Ruth League urges all leagues to have a safety plan in place for severe weather conditions. Establish specific guidelines that outline where people should go for safety and shelter, and know how much time it will take for them to reach shelter.

Safe places to take cover from lightning strikes include fully enclosed metal vehicles with the windows up, enclosed buildings, and low ground (under cover of bushes, if possible). It's not safe to be near metal objects such as flag poles, fences, light poles, and metal bleachers. Also avoid trees, hill or ridge tops, water, and open fields. Never lie flat on the ground during a lightning storm.

You should cancel practice when under either a tornado watch or warning. If you are practicing or competing when a tornado is nearby, you and your team should get inside a building if possible. If you cannot get into a building, lie in a ditch or other low-lying area or crouch near a strong building. Use your arms to protect your head and neck and instruct players to do the same.

The keys to handling severe weather are caution and prudence. Don't try to get that last 10 minutes of practice in if lightning is on the horizon. Don't continue to play in heavy rain. Many storms can strike both quickly and ferociously. Respect the weather and play it safe.

Air Pollution

Poor air quality and smog can present real dangers to your players. Both short- and long-term lung damage are possible from exposure to unsafe air. Although it's true that participating in clean air is not possible in many areas, restricting activity is recommended when the air quality ratings are lower than moderate or when there is a smog alert. Your local health department or air quality control board can inform you of the air quality ratings for your area and when restricting activities is recommended.

Responding to Players' Injuries

No matter how good and thorough your prevention program is, injuries most likely will occur. When injury does strike, chances are you will be the one in charge. The severity and nature of the injury will determine how actively involved you'll be in treating it. But regardless of how seriously a player is hurt, it is your responsibility to know what steps to take. Therefore, you must be prepared to take appropriate action and provide basic emergency care when an injury occurs.

Being Prepared

Being prepared to provide basic emergency care involves many things, including being trained in cardiopulmonary resuscitation (CPR) and first aid and having an emergency plan.

CPR and First Aid Training

Babe Ruth League recommends that all coaches receive CPR and first aid training from a nationally recognized organization such as the National Safety Council, the American Heart Association, the American Red Cross, or the American Sport Education Program (ASEP). You should be certified based on a practical test and a written test of knowledge. CPR training should include pediatric and adult basic life support and obstructed airway procedures. If you are unable to complete CPR training, make sure at least one of the coaches on your team does so.

First Aid Kit

A well-stocked first aid kit should include the following:

- Antibacterial soap or wipes
- Arm sling
- Athletic tape (one and a half inches wide)
- Bandage scissors
- Bandage strips (assorted sizes)
- Blood spill kit
- Cell phone
- Contact lens case
- Cotton swabs
- Elastic wraps (three, four, and six inches)
- Emergency blanket
- Examination gloves (latex free)
- Eye black
- Eye patch
- First aid cream or antibacterial ointment
- Foam rubber (one-eighth, one-fourth, and one-half inch)
- Insect sting kit
- List of emergency phone numbers
- Mirror
- Moleskin
- Nail clippers
- Oral thermometer (to determine if a player has a fever caused by illness)
- Penlight
- Petroleum jelly
- Plastic bags for crushed ice
- Prewrap (underwrap for tape)
- Safety glasses (for assistance in first aid)
- Safety pins
- Saline solution for eyes
- Sterile gauze pads (three-inch and four-inch squares, preferably nonstick)
- Sterile gauze rolls
- Sunscreen (SPF 30 or greater)
- Tape adherent and tape remover
- Tongue depressors
- Tooth saver kit
- Triangular bandages
- Tweezers

Adapted by permission from M. Flegel, *Sport First Aid*, 5th ed. (Champaign, IL: Human Kinetics, 2014), 20.

Emergency Plan

An emergency plan is the final step in being prepared to take appropriate action for severe or serious injuries. The plan calls for three steps:

1. Evaluate the injured player.

Use your CPR and first aid training to guide you. Be sure to keep these certifications up-to-date. Practice your skills frequently to keep them fresh and ready to use if and when you need them.

2. Call the appropriate medical personnel.

If possible, delegate the responsibility of seeking medical help to another calm and responsible adult who attends all practices and games. Write out a list of emergency phone numbers and keep it with you at practices and games, and also have them saved in your contacts list on your phone. Include the following phone numbers:

- Rescue unit
- Hospital
- Physician
- Police
- Fire department

Take each player's emergency information to every practice and game (see Emergency Information and Consent for Treatment Form at the end of chapter 2). This information includes the person to contact in case of an emergency, what types of medications the player is using, what types of drugs the player is allergic to, and so on.

Give an emergency response card (see Emergency Response Card at the end of this chapter) to the contact person calling for emergency assistance. Having this information ready should help the contact person remain calm. You must also complete an injury report form (see the end of this chapter for a sample Injury Report Form) and keep it on file for any injury that occurs.

3. Provide first aid.

If medical personnel are not on hand at the time of the injury, you should provide first aid care to the extent of your qualifications. Again, although your CPR and first aid training will guide you, you must remember the following:

- Do not move the injured player if the injury is to the head, neck, or back; if a large joint (ankle, knee, elbow, shoulder) is dislocated; or if the pelvis, a rib, or an arm or leg is fractured.

Emergency Steps

You must have a clear, well-rehearsed emergency action plan. You want to be sure you are prepared in case of an emergency, because every second counts. Your emergency plan should follow this sequence:

1. Check the player's level of consciousness.
2. Send a contact person to call the appropriate medical personnel and to call the player's parents.
3. Send someone to wait for the rescue team and direct them to the injured player.
4. Assess the injury.
5. Administer first aid.
6. Assist emergency medical personnel in preparing the player for transportation to a medical facility.
7. Appoint someone to go with the player if the parents are not available. This person should be responsible, calm, and familiar with the player. Assistant coaches or parents are best for this job.
8. Complete an injury report while the incident is fresh in your mind (see the end of this chapter for a sample Injury Report Form).

- Calm the injured player and keep others away from him as much as possible.
- Evaluate whether the player's breathing has stopped or is irregular, and if necessary, clear the airway with your fingers.
- Administer CPR as directed in the CPR certification course.
- Remain with the player until medical personnel arrive.

Taking Appropriate Action

Proper CPR and first aid training, a well-stocked first aid kit, and an emergency plan help prepare you to take appropriate action when an injury occurs. In the previous section, we mentioned the importance of providing first aid to the extent of your qualifications. Don't "play doctor" with injuries; sort out minor injuries that you can treat from those that need medical attention. Now let's look at taking the appropriate action for minor injuries and more serious injuries.

Minor Injuries

Although no injury seems minor to the person experiencing it, most injuries are neither life threatening nor severe enough to restrict participation. When these injuries occur, you can take an active role in their initial treatment.

Scrapes and Cuts   When one of your players has an open wound, the first thing you should do is put on a pair of disposable latex-free examination gloves or some other effective blood barrier. Then follow these four steps:

1. Stop the bleeding by applying direct pressure with a clean dressing to the wound and elevating it. The player may be able to apply this pressure while you put on your gloves. Do not remove the dressing if it becomes soaked with blood. Instead, place an additional dressing on top of the one already in place. If bleeding continues, elevate the injured area above the heart and maintain pressure.

2. Cleanse the wound thoroughly once the bleeding is controlled. A good rinsing with a forceful stream of water, and perhaps light scrubbing with soap, will help prevent infection.

3. Protect the wound with sterile gauze or a bandage strip. If the player continues to participate, apply protective padding over the injured area.

4. Remove and dispose of gloves carefully to prevent you or anyone else from coming into contact with blood.

For bloody noses not associated with serious facial injury, have the player sit and lean slightly forward. Then pinch the player's nostrils shut. If the bleeding continues after several minutes, or if the player has a history of nosebleeds, seek medical assistance.

COACHING TIP   You shouldn't let a fear of acquired immune deficiency syndrome (AIDS) and other communicable diseases stop you from helping a player. You are only at risk if you allow contaminated blood to come in contact with an open wound on your body, so the examination gloves that you wear will protect you from AIDS if one of your players carries this disease. Check with your league or the Centers for Disease Control and Prevention (CDC) for more information about protecting yourself and your participants from AIDS.

Strains and Sprains   The physical demands of playing baseball sometimes result in injury to the muscles or tendons (strains) or to the ligaments (sprains). When your players suffer minor strains or sprains, you should immediately apply the PRICE method of injury care:

P	Protect the player and the injured body part from further danger or trauma.
R	Rest the injured area to avoid further damage and to foster healing.
I	Ice the area to reduce swelling and pain.
C	Compress the area by securing an ice bag in place with an elastic wrap.
E	Elevate the injury above heart level to keep the blood from pooling in the area.

Bumps and Bruises Inevitably, baseball players make contact with each other and with the ground. If the force applied to a body part at impact is great enough, a bump or bruise will result. Many players continue playing with such sore spots, but if the bump or bruise is large and painful, you should take appropriate action. Again, use the PRICE method for injury care and monitor the injury. If swelling, discoloration, and pain have lessened, the player may resume participation with protective padding; if not, the player should be examined by a physician.

Serious Injuries

Head, neck, and back injuries; fractures; and injuries that cause a player to lose consciousness are among a class of injuries that you cannot and should not try to treat yourself. In these cases, you should follow the emergency plan outlined earlier in the chapter. We do want to examine more closely, however, your role in preventing and attending to heat cramps, heat exhaustion, and heatstroke. Additionally, please refer to figure 4.2 for an illustrative example of the signs and symptoms associated with heat exhaustion and heatstroke.

Heat Cramps Tough practices combined with heat stress and substantial fluid loss from sweating can provoke muscle cramps commonly known as heat cramps. Cramping is most common when the weather is hot. Depending on your location, it may be hot early in the season—which can be problematic because players may be less conditioned and less adapted to heat—or later in the season, when players are better conditioned but still not used to playing in high temperatures. A cramp—a severe tightening of the muscle—can drop players and prevent continued play. Dehydration, electrolyte loss, and fatigue are the contributing factors. The immediate treatment is to have the player cool off, replace fluids lost through activity, and slowly stretch the contracted muscle. A player may return to play later that same day or the next day provided the cramp doesn't cause a muscle strain.

Heat exhaustion

Dizziness

Headache

Fatigue

Dehydration

Profuse sweating

Mildly increased body
temperature

Nausea or vomiting

Diarrhea

Muscle cramps

Heatstroke

Dizziness

Headache

Disoriented, combative,
or unconscious

Dehydration

Hot and wet or dry skin

Markedly increased body
temperature

Nausea or vomiting

Diarrhea

FIGURE 4.2 Signs and symptoms of heat exhaustion and heatstroke.

Heat Exhaustion Heat exhaustion is a shocklike condition caused by strenuous activity combined with heat stress. This, in addition to dehydration and electrolyte depletion, does not allow the body to keep up. Symptoms include fatigue; dizziness; headache; nausea, vomiting, and diarrhea; and muscle cramps. Difficulty continuing activity, profuse sweating, and mildly increased body temperature are key signs of heat exhaustion.

A player suffering from heat exhaustion should rest in a cool, shaded, or air-conditioned area with legs propped above heart level; remove excess clothing and equipment; drink cool fluids, particularly those containing electrolytes (if not nauseated); and apply ice to the neck, back, or abdomen to help cool the body. If you believe a player is suffering from heat exhaustion, seek medical attention. Under no conditions should the player return to activity that day, and it is recommended that he does not return to activity until he has a written release from a physician.

Heatstroke Heatstroke is a life-threatening condition in which the body stops sweating and body temperature rises dangerously high due to continuation of strenuous activity in extreme temperatures. It occurs when dehydration and electrolyte depletion cause a malfunction in the body's temperature control center in the brain. Symptoms include fatigue; dizziness; confusion, irritability, or hysteria; nausea, vomiting, and diarrhea; and the feeling of being extremely hot. Signs include hot and wet or dry skin; rapid pulse and rapid breathing; and possible seizures, unconsciousness, or respiratory or cardiac arrest.

If you suspect that a player is suffering from heatstroke, send for emergency medical assistance immediately, and cool the player as quickly as possible. Remove excess clothing and equipment, and cool the player's body with cool, wet towels; by pouring cool water over him; or by placing the player in a cold bath. Apply ice packs to the armpits, neck, back, and abdomen and between the legs. If the player is conscious, give him cool fluids to drink. If the player is unconscious or falls unconscious, place him on his side to allow fluids and vomit to drain from the mouth. A player who has suffered heatstroke may not return to activity until he has a written release from a physician.

Protecting Yourself

When one of your players is injured, naturally your first concern is the player's well-being. You care about kids and providing life lessons that can be applied beyond the baseball diamond; after all, these are some of the reasons you decided to coach for your local Babe Ruth League. Unfortunately, you must also consider something else: Can you be held liable for the injury?

From a legal standpoint, a coach must fulfill nine duties. We've discussed all but planning in this chapter (planning is discussed in chapters 5 and 11). The following is a summary of your legal duties:

1. Provide a safe environment.
2. Properly plan the activity.
3. Provide adequate and proper equipment.
4. Match players appropriately.
5. Warn of inherent risks in the sport.
6. Supervise the activity closely.
7. Evaluate players for injury or incapacitation.
8. Know emergency procedures, CPR, and first aid.
9. Keep adequate records.

In addition to fulfilling these nine legal duties, you should check your Babe Ruth League's insurance coverage and your own insurance coverage to make sure these policies will properly protect you from liability.

Facilities and Equipment Checklist

On the Field

- ❏ Surfaces—proper grading (check for high or low spots); no holes; no abrasive items or rocks; no debris; no toxic substances (lime, fertilizer, and so on); no protruding wires, pipes or lines; field is not too wet or dry; field lines are well marked

- ❏ Bases—properly secured posts; no holes; bottom of home plate flat on playing surface

- ❏ Running paths and sliding zones—leveled off; no dips near bases

- ❏ Skinned areas—no unsafe wet spots or puddles

- ❏ Fencing—bottom rail properly buried; no holes or breaks; properly covered

- ❏ Dugouts—screened; roofed; bat and helmet racks installed and secured

- ❏ Pitcher's mound—proper height and grading; no holes

- ❏ Backstop—base properly buried; no holes or breaks

- ❏ Warning track—minimum 10 feet from fence; no holes; no large rocks

- ❏ Sprinklers—kept below dirt level to avoid tripping

Off the Field

Concession Stand

- ❏ In compliance with local, state, and federal codes

- ❏ Appliances in working order

- ❏ CO_2 tanks secured

- ❏ Smoke alarms and fire extinguishers working

- ❏ Barbeque grills located away from exits

- ❏ Propane tanks inspected

- ❏ Cleaners and chemicals stored away from food

- ❏ Boxes stored on shelves, off the floor, and out of walkways

- ❏ Customer doors or windows checked for safety

- ❏ Pricing signs correct

- ❏ Breaker boxes locked and grounded

- ❑ Signage posted for proper emergency first aid in prominent area
- ❑ Emergency phone numbers posted in prominent area

Bleachers (General)

- ❑ In compliance with local, state, and federal codes
- ❑ Vertical opening between guardrails, footboards, and seat boards not to exceed four inches
- ❑ Cross bracing and footings on fixed bleachers should not move
- ❑ No loose, missing, or protruding nuts and bolts
- ❑ Steps should be even and accessible
- ❑ An inch or two of a contrasting color painted across the nose thread of each step

Bleachers (Aluminum)

- ❑ Must meet American Society for Testing and Materials (ASTM) guidelines
- ❑ Must be electrically grounded
- ❑ End caps checked
- ❑ Hand and back rails checked
- ❑ Protective fencing along back and sides

Bleachers (Wood)

- ❑ Rotted and splintered wood replaced (any wood that can be easily damaged with a pointed object is suspect and should be cause for immediate repair)
- ❑ Height of single-board bleachers not to exceed six feet

Other

- ❑ Proper nettings, screens, and fencing to protect players, volunteers, and spectators during practice and games
- ❑ Well-stocked first aid kits available at all times
- ❑ Rest rooms cleaned, stocked, and in working order
- ❑ Storage sheds and facilities locked
- ❑ Playground area (ground surface and equipment), if applicable, in safe condition.

> continued

- ❑ Scoreboard in working order; properly grounded and locked

- ❑ Signage informing players, volunteers, and spectators of rules and regulations

- ❑ Signage warning of areas under construction, areas blocked off, and other hazardous areas

- ❑ Supply and location of garbage cans adequate

- ❑ Sometimes parents prefer to set up chairs and blankets in areas that are exposed to hard-hit foul balls or errant throws. Conversations or mobile devices can distract the spectators from the game action, which means they are not prepared to protect themselves or small children with them from batted or thrown balls. If a safe, official rooting section (away from the bleachers or behind fenced-in areas) cannot be set up, then rules must be established and displayed to prevent spectators from gathering in unsafe areas.

Closing for the Season

- ❑ Field maintenance equipment cleaned, repaired, or replaced

- ❑ Water pipes drained

- ❑ Sprinkler system winterized

- ❑ Perishable goods removed from the concession stand

- ❑ Concession stand winterized

From Babe Ruth League, *Coaching Youth Baseball* (Champaign, IL: Human Kinetics, 2019).

Injury Report Form

Date of injury: _____ Time: _____ a.m./p.m.

Location: _____

Player's name: _____

Age: _____ Date of birth: _____

Type of injury: _____

Anatomical area involved: _____

Cause of injury: _____

_____

_____

Extent of injury: _____

_____

_____

Person administering first aid (name): _____

First aid administered: _____

_____

Other treatment administered: _____

_____

Referral action: _____

_____

Signature of person administering first aid: _____

Date: _____

From Babe Ruth League, *Coaching Youth Baseball* (Champaign, IL: Human Kinetics, 2019).

Emergency Response Card

Be prepared to give the following information to an EMS dispatcher.

(*Note:* Do not hang up first. Let the EMS dispatcher hang up first.)

Caller's name: _____

Telephone number from which the call is being made: _____

Reason for call: _____

How many people are injured: _____

Condition of victim(s): _____

First aid being given: _____

Location: _____

Address: _____

City: _____

Directions (e.g., cross streets, landmarks, entrance access):

From Babe Ruth League, *Coaching Youth Baseball* (Champaign, IL: Human Kinetics, 2019).

Making Practices Fun and Practical

One of the basic philosophies of Babe Ruth League is to provide every youngster the opportunity to play baseball and to have fun doing so. On the surface this means we should let the kids play the games, which is important from both an enjoyment and a developmental standpoint. However, when it comes to developing young baseball players—from T-ball right up through high school—the importance of practice, even during the season, cannot be underestimated.

In the past, we have placed too much emphasis on the learning of skills and not enough on learning how to play skillfully—that is, how to use those skills in competition. The games approach—in contrast to the traditional approach—emphasizes learning what to do first, then how to do it. Moreover, the games approach lets kids discover what to do in the game, not by your telling them, but by their experiencing it. It is a guided discovery method of teaching that empowers your kids to solve the problems that arise in the game, which is a large part of the fun in learning.

On the surface, it would seem to make sense to introduce baseball using the traditional approach (by first teaching the basic skills of the sport and then the tactics of the game), but this approach has been shown to have disadvantages. First, it teaches the skills of the sport out of the context of the game. Kids may develop a great-looking swing while hitting off a tee or in soft-toss drills in practice, but they may find it difficult to get a hit in a game. This is because they do not yet understand the fundamental tactics of baseball and do not appreciate how best to use their newfound skills. Second, learning skills by doing drills outside of the context of the game is downright boring. The single biggest turnoff in sports is overorganized instruction that deprives kids of their intrinsic desire to play the game.

The games approach is taught using a four-step process. These steps are as follows:

1. Play a modified game.
2. Help players understand the game.
3. Teach the skills of the game.
4. Practice the skills in another game.

Step 1: Play a Modified Game

It's the first day of practice; some of the kids are eager to get started, while others are obviously apprehensive. Some have rarely hit a ball, most don't know the rules, and none knows the positions in baseball. What do you do?

If you used the traditional approach, you would start with a quick warm-up activity, then line the players up for a simple hitting or throwing drill and go from there. With the games approach, however, you begin by playing a modified game that is developmentally appropriate for the level of the players and also designed to focus on learning a specific part of the game.

Activities Checklist

When developing activities for your Babe Ruth team, here are a few questions that you should ask yourself:

- Are the activities fun?
- Are the activities organized?
- Are the players involved in the activities?
- Do the activities require the players to use creativity and decision making?
- Are the spaces used appropriate for the activities?
- Is the coach's feedback appropriate?
- Are there implications for the game?

Modifying the game emphasizes a limited number of situations in the game. This is one way you guide your players to discover certain tactics in the game. For instance, you may set up an infield and place a runner on first base, then hit ground balls to the infielders. The goal of the game is for the defense to prevent the runner from advancing to second base. Each time a ground ball is hit, a runner at first base will be going to second. Playing the game this way forces players to think about what they have to do to keep the runner from advancing in a variety of situations.

Step 2: Help Players Understand the Game

As your players are playing a modified game, you should look for the right spot to freeze the action, step in, and ask questions about errors that you're seeing. When you do this, you help the players better understand the objective of the game, what they must do to achieve that objective, and also what skills they must use to achieve that objective.

Asking the right questions is a very important part of your teaching. Essentially, you'll be asking your players—often literally—"What do you need to do to succeed in this situation?" Sometimes players simply need to have more time playing the game, or you may need to modify the game further—perhaps by making the playing field smaller—so that it is even easier for them to discover what they are capable of doing. It may take more patience on your part, but it's a powerful way for players to learn. For example, assume your players are playing a game in which the objective is to keep the runner on first base from advancing to second base, but they are having trouble doing so. Interrupt the action and ask the following questions:

- What are you supposed to do in this game?
- What do you have to do to keep the runner from advancing?

- Who covers the base if the ball is hit to the right side of the infield?
- Who covers second if the ball is hit to the left side?

At first, asking the right questions might seem difficult because your players have little or no experience with the game. Or, if you've learned sport through the traditional approach, you'll be tempted to tell your players how to play the game rather than wasting time asking questions. When using the games approach, however, you must resist this powerful temptation to tell your players what to do.

Instead, through the modified game and skillful questioning on your part, your players should come to the realization on their own that accurate fielding skills and tactical awareness are essential to their success in keeping runners from advancing. Just as important, rather than telling them what the critical skills are, you led them to this discovery, which is a crucial part of the games approach.

COACHING TIP If your players have trouble understanding what to do, you can phrase your questions to let the players choose between one option or another. For example, if you ask them, "What are you supposed to do when bunting?" and get an answer such as "Get the ball on the ground," then ask, "Where should you put it: first-base side or third-base side?"

Step 3: Teach the Skills of the Game

Only when your players recognize the skills they need to be successful in the game do you want to teach the specific skills through focused activities (that is, activities consisting of the skills needed to be successful in a specific game situation). This is when you use a more traditional approach to teaching sport skills—the IDEA approach—which we will describe in chapter 6. This type of teaching breaks down the skills of the game. It should be implemented early in the season so that players can begin attaining skill, which will make games more fun.

Step 4: Practice the Skills in Another Game

As a coach, you want your players to experience success as they're learning skills, and the best way for them to experience this success early on is for you to create an advantage for the players. Once the players have practiced a skill, as outlined in step 3, you can then put them in another game situation, this time changing the rules of the game slightly to create an advantage. For example, if the skill being worked on is bunting, you can change the rules to favor the bunter: If strikeouts aren't allowed or fielders aren't allowed to charge the plate until the ball gets there, this would make it easier for players to lay down successful bunts and gain confidence in their ability. Your players may concentrate more on getting the bunt down on the ground if they know they have more time to do it (instead of hurrying to get the bunt down under pressure).

We recommend first using the regular rules of the game before making changes to the number of players, the size of the field, or the rules. This sequence enables you to first introduce your players to a situation similar to what they will experience in competition, and to let them discover the challenges they face in performing the necessary skill. Then you teach them the skill, have them practice it, and put them back in another game—this time changing some aspect of the game to give them a greater chance of experiencing success.

As players improve their skills, however, you may need to again change the rules. Not allowing fielders to move until the ball crosses the plate will eventually make it too easy for your batters and won't challenge them to hone their skills. When this time comes, you can lessen the advantage—for example, by moving the fielders in a little—or you may even decide that the players are ready to practice the skill under regulation rules. The key is to set up situations where your players experience success yet are challenged in doing so. This will take careful monitoring on your part, but having kids play modified games as they are learning skills is a very effective way of helping them learn and improve.

And that's the games approach. Your players will get to play more in practice, and once they learn how the skills fit into their performance and enjoyment of the game, they'll be more motivated to work on those skills, which will help them be successful.

COACHING TIP Some baseball skills don't easily lend themselves to modified games where you can create an advantage. For example, the basic mechanics of throwing the ball or making a catch are best taught with individual attention to each player, often as players practice with a partner. Offensive tactics, as well as team defensive plays, however, are ideal for gamelike settings.

Teaching and Shaping Skills

Coaching baseball is about teaching kids how to play the game by teaching them skills, fitness, and values. It's also about "coaching" players before, during, and after games. Teaching and coaching are closely related, but there are important differences. In this chapter, we focus on principles of teaching, especially on teaching technical and tactical skills. But these principles apply to teaching values and fitness concepts as well. Armed with these principles, you will be able to design effective and efficient practices and will understand how to deal with misbehavior. Then you will be able to teach the skills and plays necessary to be successful in baseball (which are outlined in chapters 7, 8, and 9).

Teaching Baseball Skills

Many people believe that the only qualification needed to teach a skill is to have performed it. Although it's helpful to have performed it, teaching it successfully requires much more than that. And even if you haven't performed the skill before, you can still learn to teach successfully with the useful acronym IDEA:

I	Introduce the skill.
D	Demonstrate the skill.
E	Explain the skill.
A	Attend to players practicing the skill.

Introduce the Skill

Players, especially those who are young and inexperienced, need to know what skill they are learning and why they are learning it. You should therefore follow these three steps every time you introduce a skill to your players:

1. Get your players' attention.
2. Name the skill.
3. Explain the importance of the skill.

Get Your Players' Attention

Because youngsters are easily distracted, you should do something to get their attention. Some coaches use interesting news items or stories. Others use jokes. And still others simply project enthusiasm to get their players to listen. Whatever method you use, speak slightly above your normal volume and look your players in the eye when you speak.

Also, position players so they can see and hear you. Arrange the players in two or three evenly spaced rows, facing you. (Make sure they aren't looking into the sun or at a distracting activity.) Then ask whether all of them can see you before you begin to speak.

Name the Skill

More than one common name may exist for the skill you are introducing, but you should decide as a staff before the start of the season which one you'll use (and then stick with it). This will help prevent confusion and enhance communication among your players. When you introduce the new skill, call it by name several times so that the players automatically correlate the name with the skill in later discussions.

COACHING TIP You may want to write out in detail each skill you will teach. This can help clarify what you will say and how you will demonstrate and teach each skill to your players.

Explain the Importance of the Skill

As Rainer Martens, the founder of the American Sport Education Program (ASEP), has said, "The most difficult aspect of coaching is this: Coaches must learn to let athletes learn. Sport skills should be taught so they have meaning to the child, not just meaning to the coach." Although the importance of a skill may be apparent to you, your players may be less able to see how the skill will help them become better baseball players. Offer them a reason for learning the skill, and describe how the skill relates to more advanced skills.

Demonstrate the Skill

The demonstration step is the most important part of teaching a sport skill to players who may never have done anything closely resembling the skill. They need a picture, not just words. They need to see how the skill is performed. If you are unable to perform the skill correctly, ask an assistant coach, one of your players, or someone more skilled to perform the demonstration.

These tips will help make your demonstrations more effective:

- Use correct form.
- Demonstrate the skill several times.
- Slow the action, if possible, during one or two performances so players can see every movement involved in the skill.
- Perform the skill at different angles so your players can get a full perspective of it.
- Demonstrate the skill with both the right and left arms and legs.

Explain the Skill

Players learn more effectively when they're given a brief explanation of the skill along with the demonstration. You should use simple terms and, if possible, relate the skill to previously learned skills. Ask your players whether they understand your description. A good technique is to ask the team to repeat your explanation. Ask questions such as "What are you going to do first?" and "Then what?" If players look confused or uncertain, you should repeat your explanation and demonstration. If possible, use different words so your players get a chance to try to understand the skill from a different perspective.

Complex skills are often better understood when they are explained in more manageable parts. For instance, if you want to teach your players how to field a ground ball, you might take the following steps:

1. Show them a correct performance of the entire skill, and explain its function in baseball.
2. Break down the skill and point out its component parts to your players.
3. Have players perform each of the component skills you have already taught them, such as assuming the ready position and moving to the ball.
4. After players have demonstrated their ability to perform the separate parts of the skill in sequence, reexplain the entire skill.
5. Have players practice the skill in gamelike conditions.

How to Properly Run Your Drills

Before running a drill that teaches technique, do the following:
- Name the drill.
- Explain the skill or skills to be taught.
- Position the players correctly.
- Explain what the drill will accomplish.
- State the command that will start the drill.
- Identify the signal that will end the drill, such as a whistle.

Once the drill has been introduced and repeated a few times in this manner, you will find that merely calling out the name of the drill is sufficient; your players will automatically line up in the proper position to run the drill and practice the skill.

Attend to Players Practicing the Skill

If the skill you selected was within your players' capabilities and you have done an effective job of introducing, demonstrating, and explaining it, your players should be ready to attempt the skill. Some players, especially those in younger age groups, may need to be physically guided through the movements during their first few attempts. Walking unsure players through the skill in this way will help them gain confidence to perform the skill on their own.

Your teaching duties, though, don't end when all your players have demonstrated that they understand how to perform a skill. In fact, your teaching role is just beginning as you help your players improve their skills. A significant part of your teaching consists of closely observing the hit-and-miss trial performances of your players. You will shape players' skills by detecting errors and correcting them using positive feedback. Keep in mind that your positive feedback will have a great influence on your players' motivation to practice and improve their performances.

Remember, too, that some players may need individual instruction. So, set aside a time before, during, or after practice to give individual help.

COACHING TIP Many baseball skills cannot be learned sufficiently unless they are practiced over and over. As a new coach, you should try to be inventive by creating new drills that teach the same skill as an old drill does. You can then substitute the new drills every once in a while to spice up practice.

Helping Players Improve Skills

After you have successfully taught your players the fundamentals of a skill, your focus will be on helping them improve the skill. Players learn skills and improve on them at different rates, so don't get frustrated if progress seems slow. Instead, help them improve by shaping their skills and detecting and correcting errors.

Shaping Players' Skills

One of your principal teaching duties is to reward positive effort or behavior—in terms of successful skill execution—when you see it. A player makes a good hit in practice, and you immediately say, "That's the way to keep your head in there! Good swing!" This, plus a smile and a "thumbs-up" gesture, goes a long way toward reinforcing that technique in that player. However, sometimes you may have a long dry spell before you see correct techniques to reinforce. It's difficult to reward players when they don't execute skills correctly. How can you shape their skills if this is the case?

Shaping skills takes practice on your players' part and patience on yours. Expect your players to make errors. Telling the player who made the good hit that he did a good job doesn't ensure that he'll have the same success next time. Seeing inconsistency in your players' technique can be frustrating. It's even more challenging to stay positive when your players repeatedly perform a skill incorrectly or have a lack of enthusiasm for learning. It can certainly be frustrating to see players who seemingly don't heed your advice and continue to make the same mistakes.

Although it is normal to get frustrated sometimes when teaching skills, part of successful coaching is controlling this frustration. Instead of getting upset, use these six guidelines for shaping skills:

1. Think small initially.

Reward the first signs of behavior that approximate what you want. Then reward closer and closer approximations of the desired behavior. In short, use your reward power to shape the behavior you seek.

2. Break skills into small steps.

For instance, in learning to field ground balls and throw to a base, one of your players does well in getting into position and watching the ball into his glove, but he uses a flat-footed throw to the base. Reinforce the correct techniques of getting into proper position and watching the ball into the glove, and teach him how to skip forward and prepare to throw. Once he masters this, you can focus on getting him to complete the skill by pushing off the back leg after skipping forward and throwing the ball over the top.

3. Develop one component of a skill at a time.

Don't try to shape two components of a skill at once. For example, in hitting, players must begin with a proper grip, get in a comfortable and appropriate stance, and use proper mechanics in the stride and swing. Players should focus first on one aspect (grip), then on another (stance), and then another (stride and swing). Players who have problems mastering a skill often do so because they're trying to improve two or more components at once. You should help these players isolate a single component.

4. Use reinforcement only occasionally, for the best examples.

By focusing only on the best examples, you will help players continue to improve once they've mastered the basics. Using occasional reinforcement during practice allows players to have more time performing a drill rather than having to constantly stop and listen to the coach. Baseball skills are best learned through a lot of repetition, such as drills, and the coach needs to make the best use of team practice time by allowing the players to have as much training time as possible.

5. Relax your reward standards.

As players focus on mastering a new skill or attempt to integrate it with other skills, their old, well-learned skills may temporarily degenerate, and you may need to relax your expectations. For example, a player just learning how to make the pivot at second base on a double play may see a temporary decline in his throwing power because he is concentrating on his footwork. This regression will only be temporary until he has learned to combine the two skills and he gets the footwork and timing down. A similar degeneration of skills may occur during growth spurts while the coordination of muscles, tendons, and ligaments catches up to the growth of bones.

6. **Go back to the basics.**

If, however, a well-learned skill degenerates for long, you may need to restore it by going back to the basics. If necessary, players should practice the skill by using an activity where players have more time or where the playing area is made smaller to complete the technique so that they can relearn it.

COACHING TIP For older age groups or players with advanced skills, coaches can ask players to self-coach. With the proper guidance and a positive team environment, young players can think about how they perform a skill and how they might be able to perform it better. Self-coaching is best done at practice, where a player can experiment with learning new skills.

Detecting and Correcting Errors

Good coaches recognize that players make two types of errors: learning errors and performance errors. Learning errors are ones that occur because players don't know how to perform a skill; that is, they have not yet developed the correct motor pattern in the brain to perform a particular skill. Performance errors are made not because players don't know how to execute the skill, but because they have made a mistake in executing what they do know. There is no easy way to know whether a player is making learning or performance errors; part of the art of coaching is being able to sort out which type of error each mistake is.

The process of helping your players correct errors begins with you observing and evaluating their performances to determine if the mistakes are learning or performance errors. You should carefully watch your players to see if they routinely make the errors in both practice and game settings, or if the errors tend to occur only in game settings. If the latter is the case, then your players are making performance errors. For performance errors, you need to look for the reasons your players are not performing as well as they know how; perhaps they are nervous, or maybe they get distracted by the game setting. If the mistakes are learning errors, then you need to help them learn the skill, which is the focus of this section.

When correcting learning errors, there is no substitute for knowledge of the skills. The better you understand a skill—not only how it is performed correctly but also what causes learning errors—the more helpful you will be in correcting your players' mistakes.

One of the most common coaching mistakes is to provide inaccurate feedback and advice on how to correct errors. Don't rush into error correction; wrong feedback or poor advice will hurt the learning process more than no feedback or advice at all. If you are uncertain about the cause of the problem or how to correct it, you should continue to observe and analyze until you are more sure. As a rule, you should see the error repeated several times before attempting to correct it.

Correct One Error at a Time

Suppose Josh, one of your outfielders, is having trouble with his fielding. He tends to break in on the ball and often has to reverse direction while the ball goes over his head, and on the balls that he is in position to catch, he uses only one hand. What do you do?

First, decide which error to correct first, because players learn more effectively when they attempt to correct one error at a time. Determine whether one error is causing the other; if so, have the player correct that error first, because it may eliminate the other error. In Josh's case, however, neither error is causing the other. In such cases, players should correct the error that is easiest to correct and will bring the greatest improvement when remedied. For Josh, this probably means getting back quickly on balls hit over his head. If balls are constantly going over his head, he needs to be positioned deeper. If they only occasionally go over his head, he needs to break his instinct of running toward the infield on every fly ball. Once he improves his ability to judge fly balls and get in proper position, then he should work on catching the ball with two hands. Note that improvement in the first area may even motivate him to correct the other error.

Use Positive Feedback to Correct Errors

The positive approach to correcting errors includes emphasizing what to do instead of what not to do. Use compliments, praise, rewards, and encouragement to correct errors. Acknowledge correct performance as well as efforts to improve. By using positive feedback, you can help your players feel good about themselves and promote a strong desire to achieve.

When you're working with one player at a time, the positive approach to correcting errors includes four steps:

1. **Praise effort and correct performance.**

Praise the player for trying to perform a skill correctly and for performing any parts of it correctly. Praise the player immediately after he performs the skill, if possible. Keep the praise simple: "Good try," "Way to hustle," "Good form," or "That's the way to follow through." You can also use nonverbal feedback, such as smiling, clapping your hands, or any facial or body expression that shows approval. Make sure you're sincere with your praise. Don't indicate that a player's effort was good when it wasn't. Usually a player knows when he has made a sincere effort to perform the skill correctly and perceives undeserved praise for what it is—untruthful feedback to make him feel good. Likewise, don't indicate that a player's performance was correct when it wasn't.

2. Give simple and precise feedback to correct errors.

Don't burden a player with a long or detailed explanation of how to correct an error. Give just enough feedback so that the player can correct one error at a time. Before giving feedback, recognize that some players readily accept it immediately after the error; others will respond better if you slightly delay the correction. For errors that are complicated to explain and difficult to correct, you should try the following:

- Explain and demonstrate what the player should have done. Do not demonstrate what the player did wrong.
- Explain the cause or causes of the error, if this isn't obvious.
- Explain why you are recommending the correction you have selected, if it's not obvious.

3. Make sure the player understands your feedback.

If the player doesn't understand your feedback, he won't be able to correct the error. Ask the player to repeat the feedback and to explain and demonstrate how it will be used. If the player can't do this, you should be patient and present your feedback again. Then have the player repeat the feedback after you're finished.

4. Provide an environment that motivates the player to improve.

Your players won't always be able to correct their errors immediately, even if they do understand your feedback. Encourage them to "hang tough" and stick with it when corrections are difficult or when players seem discouraged. For more difficult corrections, you should remind players that it will take time and that the improvement will happen only if they work at it. Encourage those players with little self-confidence. Saying something like, "You were hitting much better today; with practice, you'll be able to keep your head in and make consistent contact," can motivate a player to continue to refine her hitting skills.

Other players may be very self-motivated and need little help from you in this area; with them you can practically ignore step 4 when correcting an error. Although motivation comes from within, you should try to provide an environment of positive instruction and encouragement to help your players improve.

A final note on correcting errors: Baseball provides unique challenges in this endeavor. How do you provide individual feedback in a group setting using a positive approach? Instead of yelling across the field to correct an error (and embarrass the player), substitute for the player who erred and make the correction on the bench. This type of feedback has several advantages:

- The player will be more receptive to the one-on-one feedback.
- The other players are still active and still practicing skills, and they are unable to hear your discussion.

- Because the rest of the team is still playing, you'll feel compelled to make your comments simple and concise—which is more helpful to the player.

This doesn't mean you can't use the team setting to give specific, positive feedback. You can do so to emphasize correct group and individual performances. Use this team feedback approach only for positive statements, though. Keep any negative feedback for individual discussions.

Dealing With Misbehavior

Players will misbehave at times; it's only natural. Following are two ways you can respond to misbehavior: through extinction or discipline.

COACHING TIP At the start of the season and at the beginning of practice when necessary, you should let players know your expectations for their behavior during practice. Announce any rules you have for practice, such as "When the whistle blows, there will be no throwing of the baseball." This helps the players realize their boundaries and your expectations.

Extinction

Ignoring a misbehavior—neither rewarding nor disciplining it—is called extinction. This can be effective under certain circumstances. In some situations, disciplining young people's misbehavior only encourages them to act up further because of the recognition they get. Ignoring misbehavior teaches youngsters that it is not worth your attention.

Sometimes, though, you cannot wait for a behavior to fizzle out. When players cause danger to themselves or others, or they disrupt the activities of others, you need to take immediate action. Tell the offending player that the behavior must stop, and that discipline will follow if it doesn't. If the player doesn't stop misbehaving after the warning, you should use discipline.

Extinction also doesn't work well when a misbehavior is self-rewarding. For example, you may be able to keep from grimacing if a youngster kicks you in the shin, but even so, that youngster still knows you were hurt. Therein lies the reward. In these circumstances, it is also necessary to discipline the player for the undesirable behavior.

Extinction works best in situations where players are seeking recognition through mischievous behaviors, clowning, or grandstanding. Usually, if you are patient, their failure to get your attention will cause the behavior to disappear. However, you must be alert that you don't extinguish desirable behavior. When youngsters do something well, they expect to be positively reinforced. Not rewarding them will likely cause them to discontinue the desired behavior.

Discipline

Some educators say we should never discipline young people, but should only reinforce their positive behaviors. They argue that discipline does not work, that it creates hostility, and that it sometimes develops avoidance behaviors that may be more unwholesome than the original problem behavior. It is true that discipline does not always work and that it can create problems when used ineffectively, but when used appropriately, discipline is effective in eliminating undesirable behaviors without creating other undesirable consequences. You must use discipline effectively, because it is impossible to guide players through positive reinforcement and extinction alone. Discipline is part of the positive approach when these guidelines are followed:

- Discipline players in a corrective way to help them improve now and in the future. Don't discipline to retaliate and make yourself feel better.

- Impose discipline in an impersonal way when players break team rules or otherwise misbehave. Shouting at or scolding players indicates that your attitude is one of revenge.

- Once a good rule has been agreed on, ensure that players who violate it experience the unpleasant consequences of their misbehavior. Don't wave discipline threateningly over their heads. Just do it, but warn a player once before disciplining.

- Be consistent in administering discipline.

- Don't discipline using consequences that may cause you guilt. If you can't think of an appropriate consequence right away, tell the player you will talk with him after you think about it. You might consider involving the player in designing a consequence.

- Once the discipline is completed, don't make players feel that they are "in the doghouse." Always make them feel that they're valued members of the team.

- Make sure that what you think is discipline isn't perceived by the player as a positive reinforcement; for instance, keeping a player out of a certain activity or portion of the training session may be just what the player wanted.

- Never discipline players for making errors when they are playing.

- Never use physical activity—running laps or doing push-ups—as discipline. To do so only causes players to resent physical activity, something we want them to learn to enjoy throughout their lives.

- Use discipline sparingly. Constant discipline and criticism cause players to turn their interests elsewhere and to resent you as well.

Play in baseball is initiated by a pitcher attempting to deliver the ball to a catcher behind home plate. This fundamental activity in the game, therefore, is a good place to start in teaching specific baseball skills and strategies.

Pitching

Any baseball coach will tell you that a big percentage of a team's success—or failure—relates to the quality of its pitchers. No other position in sports has more impact on the outcome of a game. Find a successful baseball team, and you'll typically also find a good pitching staff.

When working with young pitchers, make it clear that good pitching takes practice and that solid pitching skills are not developed by just throwing the ball. A good pitcher requires a strong and accurate throwing arm. Pitchers learn best by throwing at a target, facing a hitter in the batter's box, and trying to use a consistent, correct delivery.

Young pitchers should work on pitching controlled, consistent fastballs before trying to master other pitches. A good fastball and, perhaps, an effective change-up are the only pitches that players younger than 14 need to have. The fastball will be the fastest pitch that a player uses; any pitch that differs much in speed from the fastball is technically considered a change-up, although a true change-up should be at least 10 miles per hour slower than the fastball. Pitchers should use the fastball to throw the ball past hitters who have a slow swing. They can mix the change-up in with the fastball to get hitters off balance. When hitters expect a fastball but get a change-up instead, their body weight will shift too quickly; as a result, even if they hit the ball, they will not hit it with much force because they will usually use an arms-only swing.

Youngsters who experiment with breaking pitches, such as the curveball, often have trouble getting the ball over the plate. They also run the risk of injuring their arms by throwing these pitches incorrectly. Medical evidence suggests that throwing curveballs when the body is still developing can cause serious damage to the ligaments and muscles of the throwing arm.

Overhand Throwing Technique

Before getting into specific pitches and their grips, it's essential that you teach all your players—pitchers included—proper overhand throwing technique. To throw a baseball well, every player must use some type of grip, windup, delivery, and follow-through. The following information describes the overhand throwing technique that you should teach your players.

Grip

Players of all ages should grip the ball across the seams in the throwing hand with the index and middle fingers spaced slightly apart and the thumb under and between the top fingers (see figure 7.1a). Younger players or players with

FIGURE 7.1 Grip for the overhand throw: *(a)* standard and *(b)* modified.

smaller hands can place the first three fingers on top of the ball so that they have better control of the throw (see figure 7.1*b*). In either case, however, the ball should be held across the seams because this will cause the flight of the ball to be straighter. If players hold the ball with the seams, the ball will sometimes curve away from their target.

COACHING TIP Make sure that players are not gripping the ball too tightly or too far back in their hand. Gripping too tightly causes tension in the arm muscles and will actually slow down the speed of the throw. Holding the ball too far back in the hand has the same effect. It makes the throw become a change-up or an off-speed throw. Players should grip the ball loosely, just hard enough so that they don't drop it—as if they were holding a raw egg.

Windup

When winding up for the overhand throw, as a player starts to pull the ball out of his glove, he should begin turning his rear foot (same side as the throwing arm) so that the instep of the foot is facing the target. Tell players to imagine that they have an arrow extending straight out of their instep. To make this step with the foot, they would have to turn that arrow so that it is pointed at their target. Once this movement has been made, the player's hips should begin to rotate, and his front shoulder should point to the target.

The player then brings the throwing arm back and up. The front shoulder is turned so that it is pointed at the target. The throwing arm is extended behind the body with the wrist cocked, the elbow bent, and the fingers on the top of the ball (see figure 7.2*a*). At the same time, the player steps toward the target with

FIGURE 7.2 Overhand throw.

the front foot. Care should be taken to point the front foot directly at the target, not too much to the left or right of it. If a right-hander's foot points to the left, the shoulders won't rotate properly and won't allow for a full arm motion in the throw. If the foot points too far to the right, the player will be throwing across his body, decreasing the speed of the throw.

Delivery

When preparing to deliver the ball, the player first picks up the lead foot and strides toward the target. As the lead foot touches the ground, the player's throwing arm should be at its highest point, and the player's hips begin to turn so that the throwing-side hip drives toward the target (see figure 7.2*b*). The player's weight transfers from the back foot to the front foot as the throwing arm is brought forward just before releasing the ball. During the delivery, the palm stays facing the ground and the fingers remain on top of the ball until the arm reaches its highest point. The elbow then begins to move toward the target, forcing the forearm to lie back into a position where it can move forward and release the ball.

COACHING TIP Watch players as they throw in drills or warm-ups to make sure that their throwing elbow is even with or above their shoulder at the delivery position. The arm is much stronger in this position, and the throw will be faster. When the elbow drops below the shoulder, especially with young players, the tendency is to throw the ball in a looping arc rather than a straight line.

Follow-Through

On the follow-through, after the ball has been released, the player lets the arm follow through toward the target and then across the body so that it finishes on the opposite side from where it started (see figure 7.2c). Because of the extension of the arm toward the target, the player will have to bend his body at the waist to allow the arm to follow the proper path. As the arm is moving into the follow-through, the body weight shifts from the rear leg, to the middle of the body, and then finally to the front leg. When the weight shifts to the front leg, the rear foot should lift off the ground, which helps the arm move across the body.

Pitches and Grips

Several different grips can be used to throw a fastball, and many variations exist within those grips. The most common grips for the fastball are the four-seam grip and the two-seam grip.

COACHING TIP Teach your players that holding the ball in their fingertips as opposed to jamming it into the hand will help them get good velocity and a quicker wrist snap for control of the fastball.

Four-Seam Fastball

The four-seam grip (see figure 7.3a) is basically the same grip as discussed for the overhand throw. The index and middle fingers are placed across the seams, with the curved horseshoe part of the ball typically facing away from the thrower (remember that younger players or players with smaller hands may need to place three fingers on top of the ball for better control). The thumb is placed under the ball so that it is centered between the two fingers on the top. The four-seam fastball will spin more times than the two-seam fastball (discussed in the next paragraph), and this spin will directly affect the ball's velocity and movement.

FIGURE 7.3 Proper grip for the fastball: *(a)* four-seam grip and *(b)* two-seam grip.

The spin on a four-seam fastball will fight the force of gravity and make the pitch appear to rise (although it actually only falls at a slower rate). The batter will swing to the area where he thinks the ball is descending, but the ball stays above the bat. Although it doesn't move left or right as much as a two-seam fastball, the four-seam fastball is easier to control and should be used when the pitcher needs to throw a strike.

Two-Seam Fastball

For the two-seam grip (see figure 7.3*b*), the ball is placed in the hand so that the two fingers on the top rest on or near the seams at their narrowest point on the ball and the thumb still bisects the two fingers. The two-seam fastball will often move or "tail" in to a right-handed batter when thrown by a right-handed pitcher. When thrown well, the pitch will start out looking like a strike and then move out of the strike zone. The hitter will swing the bat to the location where he thinks the bat's sweet spot will connect with the ball, only to have the ball hit weakly off the handle instead. The two-seam fastball may even sink—because it has less spin—if thrown a certain way. Normally, if mastered, this pitch can force more ground balls from hitters.

Players can experiment with the four-seam and two-seam fastball grips by applying pressure differently with the fingers on top of the ball or by moving the fingers closer together or farther apart. Generally, the closer together the fingers are on the top of the ball, the harder the ball can be thrown. But, when the fingers are closer together, players must realize that it is more difficult to control the ball's flight. Additionally, moving the thumb underneath the ball may also make the ball act differently on the throw. You should work with your players in practice to help them find and perfect a grip that gives them the best control and the best velocity.

Change-Up

The change-up grip can be a variation of either of the fastball grips discussed previously. With the change-up, however, the ball is held deeper in the hand so that it does not come out of the hand as quickly (see figure 7.4). Older players who throw the fastball with the two fingers on top may want to place three fingers on top of the ball when they throw a change-up. This will cause the ball to be released more slowly.

The Pitching Motion

The pitching motion incorporates many of the same skills as the overhand throw introduced earlier in the chapter.

FIGURE 7.4 Proper grip for the change-up.

Windup

The pitching motion begins with the windup. This is the first movement a pitcher makes to put his body in motion. To begin the windup, the player grips the ball with the throwing hand held in the glove near the midpoint of his body. Keeping the back part of the ball-side foot in contact with the front side of the pitching rubber, the pitcher lifts his arms over his head while taking a short step behind or to the side of the rubber. Some pitchers may choose to only lift the arms slightly without bringing them over the head (see figure 7.5a).

Pivot

The pivot is the most essential part of the pitching motion. As in the basic overhand throwing motion, the instep of the foot must point toward the target before a pitch can be thrown. After the short step in the windup has been taken, the pitcher's weight should be balanced, and his eyes should be on the target. The pitcher then lifts the ball-side foot slightly and turns it parallel to the rubber so that the side of the foot near the little toe is in contact with the rubber. (*Note:* On a well-kept mound, it will most likely be unnecessary for the player to lift the foot. The pitcher will simply slide and turn the foot. Most youth league mounds, however, have holes dug in front of the rubber. If this is the case, the pitcher will have to lift the foot and place it in the hole to avoid losing balance.) At this point, the pitcher shifts his weight forward onto the ball-side foot and lifts the glove-side leg into the air so that the leg is dangling directly under the knee (see figure 7.5b). At the same time, the pitcher turns his hips and shoulders so that they rotate and point toward home plate. When these movements have been completed, the pitcher should be in a balanced position from which he can gather force and throw the pitch.

COACHING TIP To help them maintain balance, remind pitchers to concentrate on using the thigh muscles and the knee when lifting their glove-side leg. Some pitchers will lift or kick out their glove-side foot instead, throwing the body out of balance; the pitcher then has to struggle to get back to the balance point.

Stride

After the pivot and the leg lift, the pitcher must stride toward the plate with the glove-side leg. During this movement, the foot of the striding leg remains closed (for a right-handed pitcher, the foot points toward third base; a left-handed pitcher's foot points toward first). The pitcher should initiate the stride by sliding the glove-side hip toward home plate and striding the leg out. The moment before

FIGURE 7.5 Pitching motion for the fastball or change-up.

the foot lands (see figure 7.5c), it is flipped open so that it points toward the plate when it lands. When the foot opens, the hips will open, which brings the upper body and the arm through the motion. At the same time, the throwing hand is moving out of the glove, and the arm is moving into throwing position (as in the overhand throw discussed previously). When the stride foot lands, the arm should be at the top of its arc near the point of release.

The toe and heel of the striding foot should land simultaneously—in the same area with each pitch—and softly to avoid any jarring in the delivery. The front knee bends so it can absorb the impact of landing with full weight on the front foot. Keeping the knee straight causes undue stress and strain on the front leg and will disrupt a smooth delivery.

COACHING TIP The length of the pitcher's stride depends on the height of the pitcher and what feels most comfortable. Too long a stride makes the ball go high; too short a stride makes the ball go low. A long stride also causes the foot to land on the heel rather than on the front part of the foot, causing erratic pitches. Have your pitchers experiment in practice to find out what stride works best.

Delivery

An overhand delivery is the most effective throwing motion for young pitchers, just as the overhand throw is best for general throwing in the field. An overhand pitching technique ensures maximum control and puts less strain on the arm than other types of deliveries. As the pitcher releases the ball, the wrist and forearm snap downward after coming over the top, and the fingers pull down on the ball, imparting spin, as shown in figure 7.5d.

Follow-Through

A good follow-through is critical for speed and control, as well as for getting the pitcher into proper fielding position. After the release, the arm travels down across the body, and the ball-side foot pivots, lifts, and swings around to a position that will square the pitcher up to the plate (see figure 7.5e). The pitcher's eyes must remain on the target, and the glove should remain in front of the chest in preparation to field any balls hit back to the mound.

COACHING TIP As a coach, you should closely monitor the technique, type, and number of pitches your players throw in both practices and games. Your league should have a maximum pitch count or standards for the number of innings a pitcher can pitch in a week, but you shouldn't automatically push your pitchers to the limit. Watch them closely (often the first sign of fatigue is a drop of the throwing elbow on pitches), and relieve them if they complain of tightness or soreness in their throwing arm or if you notice them tiring.

The Stretch Position

With older players or in leagues that allow baserunners to take leadoffs, coaches should teach pitchers how to throw out of the stretch position when there are runners on base. Because the time it takes to deliver the ball from the stretch position (also known as the *set position*) is less than the time used for the windup, the stretch position allows the pitcher to hold runners closer. Plus, in the windup position, pitchers cannot throw to first base once they have started their windup motion because this would be considered committing a balk.

The stretch position begins with the body turned perpendicular to the pitching rubber. The pitcher's feet are shoulder-width apart, with the ball-side foot in contact with the rubber and the other foot parallel to it. The pitcher takes his sign from the catcher and then brings his hands together in the middle of his body (see figure 7.6). From this position, the pitcher can either throw a pitch home or attempt a pickoff at first base. Coaches must be sure to teach pitchers that they can't just bring their hands together and quickly throw. Rule books state that a pitcher must come to a complete stop in the stretch position before throwing home.

FIGURE 7.6 Stretch position.

If a right-handed pitcher chooses to throw to first base, he can use one of two ways to move his right foot off the rubber before throwing. The first way is to step back off the rubber with the right foot, then pivot, step to first with the left foot, and throw. The second way is much quicker, but it takes far more practice and coordination to learn to do well, especially for younger players. In this method, the pitcher takes a short jab step toward third with the right foot, then pivots, steps to first, and throws. A left-handed pitcher who chooses to throw to first has a much easier method than a right-handed pitcher does. When in the stretch position, all the lefty has to do is lift the right leg, step to first, and throw. This movement, though simple, often confuses baserunners because the motion—until the right foot steps to first—is the same as the one that the left-handed pitcher uses to throw home.

If a right-handed pitcher chooses to make a pitch to the plate, he may prefer to take a very short stride to start his momentum. A short stride quickens the time of delivery to the plate and gives the catcher more time to throw the ball to second base on a steal. Right-handed pitchers who use a short stride—often called a *glide stride*—do not get as much of the body into a throw as those who use a longer stride. Left-handed pitchers do not have to worry about a short stride because of the advantage they have in being able to face the baserunner at first and hold the runner with deceptive leg kicks. Several techniques can be used to shorten the stride in the set position. One way is to start the motion by bringing the front knee swiftly toward the back knee and then striding toward home as the throwing arm begins its action. Another way to quicken the movement is to keep more weight on the back leg, making it easier to lift the front leg quickly and throw the pitch. The second method makes it more difficult for a pitcher to throw to first because most of the weight is on the ball-side leg, which makes it almost impossible to step back off the rubber. Whatever method pitchers choose to quicken their motion in the stretch, they must still use good overhand throwing technique and should not rush the delivery.

PITCHER'S BALANCE DRILL

Description

Pitchers pair up and stand 25 to 45 feet apart, depending on the age group. Each pair should be facing each other. (For younger age groups, you should have all players participate, not just pitchers.) One player will act as the catcher, assuming a catcher's position in front of a moveable rubber base. The other player will act as the pitcher, assuming a balanced stretch position with the hands together in the center of the body. On the coach's command, pitchers move through the correct pitching motion—lifting the glove-side leg to the balance point, lifting the glove-side knee a little more, drawing the ball out of the glove, beginning the overhand pitching motion, striding toward the catcher, and completing the throw. Players can be challenged by having the catcher move the glove to different positions (inside, outside, high, low, and so forth). Repeat 10 to 15 times and then switch positions.

BULL'S-EYE

Description

Divide your players into two teams, and assign a catcher for each team. (With older players, only the pitchers should participate in this game.) The coach and an assistant or another player will position themselves behind each catcher to call balls and strikes. The pitchers line up in two single-file lines (at the appropriate pitching distance from the catcher). The first pitcher in line for each team makes five pitches to his catcher. After five pitches, the pitcher gives way to the next pitcher and takes a position at the end of the line. Continue until each pitcher has had two turns. The team with the highest number of strikes wins.

Variations

- To make the game easier for younger or less skilled players, shorten the pitching distance (even if it is shorter than your league's specified field dimensions).
- To make the game more challenging for older or more skilled players, make pitchers throw strikes to certain locations (e.g., low and to one side of the plate).

Catching

As mentioned previously, simply stated, baseball is a game of throw and catch. Although throwing is decidedly the more difficult skill in this pair, catching should not be overlooked when teaching basic skills. During the course of a game, there will be several dozen opportunities for players to catch a ball. Each one of these opportunities will be important to the outcome of the game, because if mishandled, they could lead to a runner being safe or a run scoring. All players on a team must learn how to catch the ball properly. This will include catching fly balls, catching ground balls, and catching a throw from another player (all covered in chapter 8). But one position has to catch more balls than any other—appropriately enough, this is the catcher.

Catching Pitches

Because catchers have to catch the ball in a much more restrictive body position than any other player, they must develop some highly specialized skills. Catchers must not only catch the pitch, but they must also try to catch it in a way that makes it look like a strike. In age groups where stealing is allowed, they must learn to drop down and block a pitch with their bodies to keep it from getting past them. Catchers also need to learn the skills necessary to quickly get up from their catching position and throw the ball to the bases.

Basic Position

In the basic catching position, which is used when no runners are on base, the catcher assumes a comfortable crouch about two feet behind the plate. He

FIGURE 7.7 Basic position for catchers.

holds the glove out as a throwing target for the pitcher and places the throwing hand behind the back (see figure 7.7). The catcher should be relaxed, and the knees should be completely bent, with the buttocks resting on the back of the calves. The upper body should be leaning forward slightly so that the chest is over the knees. The catcher can move the body and the target around the plate to give the pitcher an inside or outside target. The legs are shoulder-width apart, and the catcher keeps his weight evenly distributed on the feet so he is ready to move in any direction for a poorly thrown ball. The catcher must stay low in his crouching position until receiving the pitch in order to avoid being hit by the swing of the batter and to allow the umpire to see the ball as it crosses the plate. When catching the ball, the catcher should "give" with the ball by bringing the glove slightly closer to the body; he should not reach the glove out toward the ball. The fingers of the glove hand should be up or to the side when catching pitches in the strike zone. The only time the catcher's fingers should point down is when catching a ball just above the ground or when blocking a ball. Younger players should strive to catch the center of the ball to help ensure that they make the catch. As they become more proficient in their skill, older players should learn how to catch the sides of the ball so that they can frame pitches in the strike zone.

From this basic crouching position, the catcher can catch pitches several different ways, depending on where the pitch is located when it reaches the catcher:

- When a pitch is thrown in the dirt just in front of the catcher, the catcher should drop both knees to the ground and slide into the ball. With the back side of the glove on the ground, the catcher should place the glove between the legs to execute the block (see figure 7.8a). Bowing the back and bringing the chin down to the chest protects the throat area and helps the catcher keep the eyes on the ball.

- When a ball is pitched in the dirt to either side of the catcher, the catcher should try to move his body into a position in front of the ball in order to block it and keep it out in front of the plate. For example, if a ball is thrown in the dirt to the catcher's left, he should slide to his left, moving

FIGURE 7.8 Catching from the basic position: (a) blocking a ball in the dirt in front of the catcher, (b) blocking a ball in the dirt to the side of the catcher, and (c) catching a ball pitched high and wide.

his left knee in the direction of the ball; he should then drop to both knees and keep the ball in the center of the body (see figure 7.8b). The opposite technique would be used on a ball to the right side. If the ball is thrown in the dirt far to the catcher's right or left, he may need to take a step toward the ball before dropping to both knees and blocking the ball in the center of the body. For example, if the ball is thrown far to the catcher's right, the catcher would take a step with the right foot and the left leg would drag behind while the glove moves between the legs.

- When a ball is pitched high or very wide, the catcher must be able to rise up quickly from the crouch—or even jump—to try to get the glove on the ball (see figure 7.8c). On this type of pitch, it is not as important to keep the body in front of the ball; the catcher should make every effort to just catch it.

Up Position

The up position is used by catchers when there are runners on base. This position will allow the catcher to receive the pitch and throw to a base quickly. In the up position, the catcher's feet should be more than shoulder-width apart, with the knees bent. The glove-side foot should be slightly in front of the throwing-side foot (a good measure of this is that the toes of the throwing-side foot should be even with the instep of the glove-side foot), and the toes should be pointed out slightly. In the up position, the catcher does not lower the buttocks as far down as he would in the basic position, but only low enough so that the thighs are nearly parallel to the ground (see figure 7.9). Also, the catcher's throwing hand should be placed behind the glove to make it easier to get the ball out of the glove in case of a steal. The thumb of the throwing hand should be placed in the fist to protect against injury from foul tips. The catcher should extend the glove hand away from the body, providing a large target area for the pitcher.

In youth leagues that permit stealing, whenever there are runners on base, the catcher should catch any pitch near or in the strike zone from the up position. When a runner attempts a steal, the catcher should lean into the ball with the upper body just before catching it, making sure not to come forward too soon, which could lead to an interference call if the batter swings and hits the catcher. For the same reason, the catcher should not reach out with the glove; he should wait

FIGURE 7.9 Up position for catchers.

until the ball comes to him. After catching the pitch, the catcher should quickly take a step with the glove-side leg toward the base where the catcher is throwing, making sure to turn the rear foot so the instep is facing the target (as discussed previously in Overhand Throw). The catcher then rotates the shoulders to be parallel to the batter's box, brings the glove hand back to a position past the middle of the body, and reaches into the glove with the throwing hand. The catcher pulls the ball out of the glove and makes the throw by stepping toward the target base with the glove-side foot, transferring weight from the back leg to the front leg. In the follow-through, the throwing hand is brought down to the opposite knee. The main difference between the catcher's throw and the basic overhand throw is that the catcher, instead of bringing the hand down out of the glove, needs to bring the ball immediately up to the top of the throwing arc, similar to when making a snap throw. This saves time and enables the catcher to make the throw more quickly.

CATCHING DRILL

Description

The coach (or a player for older age groups) stands about 15 feet in front of the catcher with a bucket of soft balls or tennis balls. The catcher should assume the basic catching position without a glove. The coach tosses underhand throws to the catcher at various locations in the strike zone. After catching the ball, the catcher should drop it down to his side and prepare to catch the next throw. After 10 to 15 throws, the catcher will use a glove, and the drill is repeated using real baseballs.

BACKSTOP

Description

Play on a field appropriate for the age group. Three players participate in this game—a catcher, a runner, and a fielder. The coach acts as the feeder. You can separate any one of the following catcher skills into a separate drill, or you can perform all five as one. The procedure for each skill is as follows:

- *Blocking pitches.* The coach throws three wild pitches in the dirt in front of the catcher. The pitch must be within reach of the catcher (not too far to the side or over the catcher's head). The catcher attempts to block each pitch. Award one point to the catcher for each successful block.

- *Throwing out runners.* The fielder plays shortstop. The runner is on first and tries to steal second as the coach pitches. The catcher throws to the shortstop covering second, who tries to tag the runner out. Award one point to the catcher for each throw to second that arrives in time to get the runner out (the point is awarded even if the shortstop drops the ball at second or misses the tag).

- *Covering the plate.* The runner is on third base. The coach throws or hits a ground ball to the fielder, who is playing shortstop. As this is done, the runner breaks for home and tries to score. For older age groups, the shortstop throws to the catcher, who blocks the plate and attempts to tag out the runner. For younger age groups, the catcher is positioned in front of the plate to make a force-out. The runner does not have to slide. Award one point to the catcher for each successful tag or force play at home.

- *Fielding a bunt and throwing to first base.* The runner is at home, and the fielder is at first base. The coach rolls a bunt down the first- or third-base line, and when the ball leaves the hand, the runner heads for first base. The catcher, starting from a crouched position, springs up as the ball is rolled and attempts to throw the runner out. Award one point to the catcher for each out at first (if the ball arrives in time to get the runner out, award the point even if the fielder at first base drops the ball).

- *Catching a foul pop-up.* The coach hits or throws high foul pop-ups near home plate. The catcher, starting from a crouched position, tracks the pop-up and attempts to catch the ball. Award one point to the catcher for each caught pop-up.

Variations

- To make fielding a bunt more challenging for older or more skilled players, the coach can roll the bunts from behind the catcher through his legs so that the catcher is forced to react without watching the coach's arm.

- To make blocking pitches more challenging for older or more skilled players, place a runner on first base who must attempt to run to second whenever the ball is thrown in the dirt. The catcher must then recover the ball and try to throw out the runner.

- To make blocking pitches easier for younger or less skilled players, the coach can point in the direction that the ball will be thrown before throwing it.

Playing defense is part instinct, part effort, and part technique. Players can improve their instincts by learning proper technique, practicing plays, and repeating what they've learned. This chapter focuses on the defensive technical and tactical skills that your players must learn in order to succeed in youth baseball. Again, remember to use the IDEA approach to teaching skills—introduce, demonstrate, and explain the skill, and attend to players as they practice the skill (see chapter 6). This chapter also ties directly into the season and practice plans in chapter 11, describing the technical skills and team tactics that you'll teach at practices outlined there. If you aren't familiar with baseball skills, you may find it helpful to watch a video so you can see the skills performed correctly.

The information in this book is limited to baseball basics. As your players advance in their skills, you will need to advance your knowledge as a coach. You can do this by learning from your experiences, watching and talking with more experienced coaches, and studying resources on advanced skills.

Defensive Technical Skills

The team with the best hitters won't necessarily win the game if their pitching is weak and their defense is poor. Especially in youth competition, teams with strong pitching and defense have more success. Much of your practice time should focus on the defensive aspects of the game, because doing so will yield greater results for your team in the long run.

Throwing

When the ball is hit by the batter, a fielder must catch the ball and then throw to another fielder who must also catch it. Since so much of the defensive game relies on the ball being thrown and caught, teaching fielders proper throwing should be at the top of every coach's to-do list.

When throwing, accuracy is more important than speed. For example, even if a shortstop fields a ball and throws hard to first base, if the throw is not accurate, the runner will probably be safe. Many players throw wildly in their attempts to put some zip on the ball or rush their throws after fielding the ball, causing them to miss their target. Thus, players need to use good throwing technique every time they throw a baseball, even when they are under pressure. Although there are many ways to throw, only a few methods of throwing will allow a player to be successful in baseball. We already covered the basic overhand throw in chapter 7, but a coach should also teach players the crow hop and the snap throw.

COACHING TIP Encourage players to always look directly at a target when throwing. This helps focus their attention and guide the throwing arm. They should never throw to another player, but rather should pick out a spot on the other player (e.g., the glove, chest, or shoulder) and throw to that target. Also, they should not watch the runner because doing so distracts them from the target.

Crow Hop

Because of the distances involved in most throws from the outfield, an outfielder needs to learn the crow hop, a move that uses the body to provide additional power in the throw. Many players throw strictly with the arm, which greatly restricts how far they can throw and leads to arm injuries. The fundamentals of the crow hop are basically the same as for the overhand throw, except the hop allows the outfielder to quickly shift the weight back and gather momentum in order to use the body as well as the arm in the throw.

To execute the crow hop when throwing the ball, the fielder's first step should be a forceful jump upward and forward with the ball-side, or back, leg (right leg for a right-handed thrower) after he catches the ball. This first step propels the fielder forward (see figure 8.1a), and then he takes a long stride with the opposite leg, enabling the body to gain momentum and help the player make a stronger throw. The motion, which resembles a crow hopping on one leg, actually forces the outfielder's body into action so that he can get more push off of his back leg and can get almost a running start to the throw. During the hop, the player's shoulders rotate into throwing position with the front shoulder pointed at the target, and the player brings the throwing arm down to begin the throwing motion (see figure 8.1b). After the hop is completed, the arm should be nearly at its highest point above the shoulder; the player then executes the throw, shifting the weight forward to the front foot (see figure 8.1c) as in a normal overhand throw.

FIGURE 8.1 Crow hop.

Snap Throw

For throwing short distances, the snap throw is a better choice than the sidearm throw. When throwing the ball a short distance, the player cannot throw the ball as hard, and the snap throw lessens the chances of a bad throw. At higher levels, this is the throw used in rundowns.

The grip for the snap throw is the same as the grip for the overhand throw. The fingers stay on top of the ball; however, the hand does not face away from the thrower.

When winding up for the snap throw, the player brings the ball directly up above the throwing-side shoulder, with the arm bent at a 90-degree angle (see figure 8.2*a*). Unlike the overhand throw, the arm motion for the snap throw involves very little arc. The shoulders remain level, and the ball faces the target. The footwork on the snap throw is the same as for the overhand throw, except the player does not have to use his lower body as much because the throw is shorter.

When initiating the delivery of the snap throw, the player brings the throwing arm forward by moving the forearm and wrist toward the target (i.e., the player he is throwing to). The player then extends the throwing arm toward the target—aiming at the player's chest—and snaps the wrist downward, releasing the ball (see figure 8.2*b*).

On the follow-through for the snap throw, the player's arm should be close to parallel to the ground, with the hand and fingers pointed toward the target, as shown in figure 8.2*b*. The hand and arm should not move across the body or

FIGURE 8.2 Snap throw.

Sidearm Throw

At the youth level, you should correct your players when they bring their arm too far away from their body in the delivery. This often results in the use of the sidearm throw and is a sign of a tired arm. Your players should be taught to use the overhand throw, because the overhand throw will give them greater control and accuracy. Conversely, using a sidearm throw can lead to bad throwing habits, wildness, and undue strain on young elbows. A player should use the sidearm throw only when there is no other choice or when throwing to a base from a short distance. Improper throwing technique at an early age can also lead to bad throwing habits and injury later in a player's career.

The best way to monitor throwing technique is to watch players during warm-up. If you see them using improper mechanics or lapsing into a sidearm or three-quarter-arm motion, you should immediately show them the correct grip, windup, delivery, and follow-through of the overhand throwing technique.

follow through too far past a point parallel to the ground, because this will force the ball to go wide of the target or go too low. Additionally, since this throw is usually used for short distances, the player only has to take a short stride with the lead foot toward the target. The throw can even be made while on the run—as in a rundown situation—or without even moving the feet.

THROWING DRILL

Description

Players are grouped in pairs; they sit on the ground in two lines facing each other, spread far enough apart so that errant throws will not cause injury. Players sit yoga style with their legs crossed and feet tucked in underneath. It is not necessary to use a glove in this drill. One player in each pair has a ball (for older players, real baseballs can be used, but players should be cautioned not to throw hard; for younger players, we suggest using softer balls, such as rag-type balls). The player with the ball starts with both hands together, as if he has the ball in his glove. On the coach's command, the player uses proper throwing motion and technique to throw softly to his partner. Coaches can use a number system of commands to isolate specific segments of the throwing motion, such as 1) take the ball out of the glove; 2) bring the ball down; 3) move it up into throwing position; and 4) throw. Players repeat the drill, throwing back and forth.

Catching Throws

During the course of a game, players will have to catch balls thrown to them from other players. This might happen when they are covering a base or serving as a cutoff player on a relay throw. In either case, many of the same principles of catching apply. To catch a throw, the player must face the thrower. The player's feet should be positioned slightly more than shoulder-width apart, and the knees should be bent (if covering a base, an infielder must first sprint to the bag and get into position). Keeping his eyes on the ball, the player should move into a position so that his chest will be in line with the flight of the ball. The player's hands should be held together, thumb to thumb, and should be ready, relaxed, and extended slightly from the body. The player's elbows should be bent and pointing toward the ground. The glove should be positioned according to the flight of the ball:

- If the ball is below the waist, the fingers and the palm of the glove hand should be pointed down with the mitt fully open (see figure 8.3a).
- If the ball is chest high, the fingers and the palm of the glove should be pointing out, with the thumb pointing to the sky (see figure 8.3b).
- If the ball is above the chest, the fingers should point toward the sky (see figure 8.3c).

As the ball is caught, the player bends the elbows slightly to absorb the force of the throw; he watches the ball into the glove, squeezing it to keep it inside. The player should catch the ball in or near the webbing of the glove because the force of the throw will almost close the glove automatically. If the ball is caught in or near the webbing, the player won't make the mistake of closing the glove with his fingers before the ball is in the glove. After the catch, the player should immediately grip the ball with the throwing hand (using the correct overhand throwing grip as discussed in chapter 7).

Players will often have to make catches when covering a base, and they need to be aware of certain things, depending on which base they are covering.

FIGURE 8.3 Catching a throw that is (a) below the waist, (b) at the chest, and (c) above the chest.

Covering First Base

Besides the catcher, the first-base player will probably catch more balls than any other player. And like the catcher, not all of the balls thrown toward him will be perfect strikes. Because the first-base player may have to adjust to all sorts of throws—high, low, wide, and so on—the player at that position must be especially good at catching throws. If the ball is hit to another player in the infield, the first thing the first-base player must do is move from his fielding position (three or four steps from the base) and get into a position to cover the base. The first-base player should sprint to the bag, turn, and then face the fielder who will be throwing the ball to him. He should assume an athletic position with the feet shoulder-width apart and the knees bent. Once the ball is in the air, the first-base player should step back and touch the bag with the throwing-side heel, keeping the glove-side leg steady. As the ball nears first base, the player should step toward it with the glove-side foot and stretch for it with the glove. If the ball can be caught in the air, the player should wait until the last possible moment before stretching for the ball; once the glove-side foot is committed in a certain direction, it is more difficult to make an adjustment if the throw is off line. In other words, the player should not commit to the bag (also known as stretch) too early. Players should also be careful not to plant their foot on top of the base because that would invite injury. After catching the ball, the player comes off the bag in position to throw, if necessary.

Pitchers must be aware that any time the ball is hit to their left side, their first move should be toward first base in case they need to cover the base. The first-base player will often field the ball and not be in a position to run back to the base and tag it for the force-out. In these situations, the pitcher has to cover the base. If he does not move toward first automatically each time a ball is hit to his left, he will not be able to get to the base in time. To get into good position to cover first base, the pitcher should first take a step or two directly at the foul line and then run diagonally to and eventually parallel to the line when he nears the base. As he approaches the base, his focus should be on the base and the ball, but when he is closer to the base, the focus should only be on the ball. While running, the pitcher extends his glove and gives the fielder a good target. To make this play work well, the first-base player must throw the ball so that the pitcher catches it one or two steps before touching the base. After catching the ball, the pitcher should step on the nearest inside portion of the base.

Covering Second Base

Besides the force play and the double play, there are two other instances when fielders must cover second base—on a steal and on a throw from the outfield. On a steal, the shortstop should get to the base ahead of the runner. The fielder should stand with the glove-side foot near the back corner of the base and their chest facing more toward first base than home plate. The fielder should assume an athletic position with the knees bent and the glove and throwing hand outstretched awaiting the throw from the catcher. As he catches the ball, he should grasp it firmly and swoop the glove down on the runner in a V fashion—down for the tag and then up and out of the way so that the ball is not knocked out of the glove. Of course, if the throw is off line, the fielder should not hold this position; instead, he should move quickly to catch the ball and stop it from going into the outfield. On a throw from the outfield, the second-base player or shortstop should position himself on the side of the base nearest the throw. The fielder should await the throw in much the same manner as in the steal, but when receiving a throw from the outfield, the fielder may have to quickly spin around to tag an advancing runner.

Covering Third Base

The techniques for covering third are similar to those for covering second. On a throw from an outfielder, the third-base player should await the throw on the outfield side of the base. On steal attempts, the positioning of the third-base player depends on where he is on the field when the ball is pitched. If playing behind the base, the third-base player should hustle toward the outfield side of the base to get the throw from the catcher. If playing in front of the base on the pitch, the third-base player should drop his throwing-side foot back toward the base, and he should try to get back to the base so that his glove-side foot makes the final step. In this position, if the throw is good, the player would catch the ball backhanded and try to make a swoop tag on the runner. If the throw is off line, the player must get his body in front of the ball and block it somehow, because if it gets past third base, a run will score.

COACHING TIP   At the youth level, you will want to teach players a method of covering bases on tag plays that limits the chances of collision and injury (such as the methods described in the previous sections). As players' skills increase, they can begin to block the base with their body as they make the tag on the runner, as long as they have the ball in their possession before the runner gets to the base. But for younger age groups, because of their lack of skill, strength, and knowledge of the sport, this would be a dangerous method to teach.

CATCHING THROWS DRILL

Description

Players are divided into two groups; one group lines up in left field, and the other lines up in right field. For each group, a tosser takes a position about 15 feet in front of the line, facing the line. On the coach's command, the first player in each line steps about 5 feet to the right of the line and assumes the proper catching position (as described in Catching Throws). The tosser throws a moderate-speed underhand throw to the player. As the ball is thrown, the tosser calls out a shortened form of one of the basic techniques of good catching—such as "throwing foot," "two hands," or "chest." The tosser makes sure that the player reacts accordingly (for "throwing foot," for example, the player should catch the ball with most of his weight positioned on his throwing-side foot when the ball enters the glove). After the catch, the player should pull the ball out of the glove, get into a good overhand throwing position, and "freeze." The player then gently tosses the ball back to the tosser and hustles to the end of the line as the next player steps out into position. As the players become more proficient, the tossers can move farther back, throw harder, and make the players do things faster. Repeat as many times as necessary.

Fielding Ground Balls

Another type of catching that players must become skilled at is fielding ground balls. Because these are hit balls, they can sometimes be traveling much faster than a thrown ball, so it is even more crucial that good catching techniques are used by fielders; otherwise, the chances of an error are multiplied.

Ready Position

Before a ball is pitched, all fielders except the catcher and the pitcher should assume the ready position. In this stance, the player's feet should be slightly wider than shoulder-width apart, with the knees bent and the weight over the balls of the feet (see figure 8.4). The player's head should face the area near home plate. The hands should hang low between the legs, with the glove open wide. From this ready position, the player can get a good jump on the ball and move quickly in the direction it is hit.

Moving to the Ball

When a ground ball is hit in a player's direction, he should move to the ball, keeping his glove-side shoulder to the right of the ball if he is right-handed (or to the left of the ball if he is left-handed). Leading with the glove, the player stays low and gets into a position where his body

FIGURE 8.4 Ready position for fielding ground balls.

is in front of the ball. This can be best accomplished by taking a quick crossover step in the direction of the ball (if the ball is hit to the left or right of the fielder). The fielder must then get his body under control when the ball is about 15 feet away so that he can drop into fielding position. To do this, a right-handed fielder takes a step with his throwing-side foot toward the ball and lowers his body into fielding position; when the next step is taken with the glove-side foot, the feet are more than shoulder-width apart, and the ball is centered on the body. This technique is an important key to good fielding. Many fielders drop down too late and don't have a chance to get into fielding position. Some never drop down at all and try to field the ball on the run.

Players should judge the speed and spin of the ball to determine where they need to move for good fielding position. With practice, players will learn to anticipate where the ball will bounce nearest to them and then move there to catch the ball. It's best to stay low and catch the ball on a low hop, near the glove, rather than an in-between hop a few to several feet in front of the glove because in-between hops are much more difficult to gauge. Therefore, players need to learn to charge the ball—move toward it—to get that low hop. It's much easier to field a ball when moving toward it than when rocking back on the heels and moving away from it.

Fielding the Ball

After moving to the ball, a player must get into the proper fielding position to field the ground ball. When the player moves his glove-side foot forward to center the body on the ball, the feet should be more than shoulder-width apart, with the toes pointed straight ahead. The throwing-side foot should be aligned slightly behind the glove-side foot so that the toes of the throwing-side foot are

FIGURE 8.5 Fielding a ground ball.

even with the instep of the other foot (see figure 8.5). The knees should be bent and the buttocks lowered to knee level. The player's back should be almost parallel to the ground, and both arms should be outstretched in front of the body. The back of the fielder's glove should be on the ground with the throwing hand either above it or alongside it. The fielder's eyes should be focused on the ball. When the ball arrives, the player should watch it into the glove and then trap it with the throwing hand, as shown in figure 8.5. The player then cushions the ball toward his body with soft hands, bringing the hands to the belt area (this is called *funneling the ball*) as he moves into throwing position.

COACHING TIP Players often have problems fielding ground balls because they try to bend for them with their back instead of their knees. This results in the player's hands being too far under his body. When this happens, the player won't be able to watch the ball all the way into the glove because his eyes will still be focused out in front of him and the ball will be underneath him. Remind your players that the ball is quicker than the eye.

Fielding Ground Balls in the Outfield

Outfielders are your team's last line of defense, and they must be able to field ground balls that get through the infield. Outfielders can use three fielding techniques to catch a ground ball:

- **Block.** This technique is used when there are no runners on base, when the ground is very bumpy, or when there's no chance of throwing a runner out. The outfielder runs to get behind the ball, drops to the throwing-side knee, puts the back of the glove on the ground, and fields the ball between the legs (see figure 8.6a). This is the safest way to field a ground ball to the outfield.

- **Scoop.** This technique is for a do-or-die situation in which the tying or winning run is attempting to score and the outfielder must make a quick throw to the infield. It's the riskiest method of fielding an outfield grounder and should be used only in situations where the game will be lost if the fielder doesn't get the ball in quickly. The outfielder runs at the ball and scoops it up with the glove while on the move. The ball should be fielded to the outside of the glove-side leg just as the glove-side foot hits the ground (see figure 8.6b). The player then crow hops off the throwing-side foot (as shown in figure 8.1) to make the throw.

- **Infield style.** This technique is used when there's a chance to throw the runner out. The outfielder gets behind the ball and fields it like an infielder, with soft hands. The player must keep the body behind the ball to help block it if it takes a bad hop (see figure 8.6c).

FIGURE 8.6 Ground ball fielding techniques for outfielders: *(a)* blocking, *(b)* scooping, and *(c)* infield style.

Skip-and-Throw

The skip-and-throw technique will help your players get rid of the ball quickly after they've fielded it. While cushioning the ball into the glove, as discussed previously, the player lines up the glove-side shoulder and hip with the throwing target (see figure 8.7*a*). With eyes focused on the target, the player skips forward and prepares to throw (see figure 8.7*b*). As the throwing hand leaves the glove, the arm extends down and back in a comfortable, relaxed position (see figure 8.7*c*). Pushing off the back leg, the player then throws over the top, moving the throwing shoulder and arm forward quickly (see figure 8.7*c*). A strong wrist snap at the point of release will result in better accuracy, or if the player is close to the base being thrown to, a snap throw might be used. To follow through on

FIGURE 8.7   Skip-and-throw.

the throw, the player points the throwing-side shoulder toward the target and lifts the back leg off the ground. The player's momentum should be forward in the direction of the throw (see figure 8.7*d*).

Forehand and Backhand Plays

There may be some times, especially on hard-hit balls, when it might not be possible for the infielder to get behind the ball to field it. In these cases, a forehand or backhand stop might be necessary for the player to get the glove behind the ball when the player can't move the entire body there in time. In the forehand play, the fielder stops the ball on the glove side of the body. For a right-hander, this involves pivoting toward the ball while staying low to the ground, using a crossover step with the right leg in the direction of the ball, sprinting to the ball, and then stepping out with the glove-side leg to field the ball just in front of the throwing-side foot (see figure 8.8*a*).

For the backhand, the fielder stops the ball on the throwing-arm side. For a right-hander, as in the forehand play, the fielder starts by pivoting toward the ball while staying low to the ground. She then executes a crossover step with the glove-side leg while reaching across the body with the glove-side arm and fielding the ball in front of the left foot. As the fielder stretches the arm toward the ball, the glove should be turned so the pocket is facing the ball, with the fingers pointing downward (see figure 8.8*b*).

FIGURE 8.8 The *(a)* forehand and *(b)* backhand catch.

🌀 FIELDING GROUND BALLS DRILL

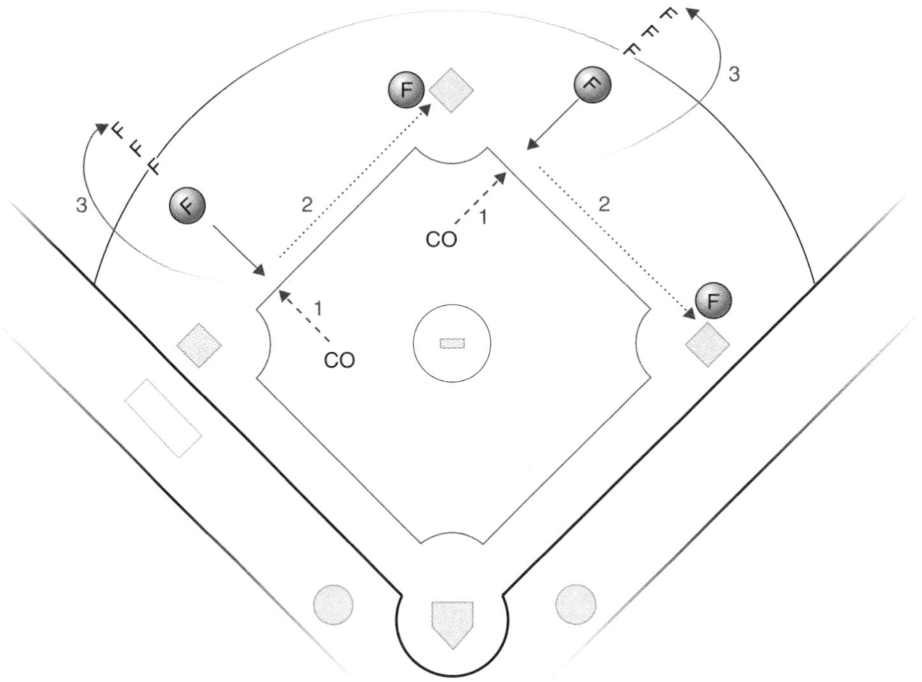

FIGURE 8.9 Fielding ground balls drill.

Description

Put one player at second base and one at first base as shown in figure 8.9. (You can have a second player at each base so that players can take turns receiving throws.) Divide the rest of your players into two single-file lines, one at the third-base position and one at the second-base position. Two coaches should be in the middle of the infield with a bucket of balls. The coaches will roll or hit ground balls to the first player in each line, who will field the ball, make a throw, and then go to the back of the line. The fielder at third base will throw to the receiver on second base, while the fielder at the second base position will throw to first base. The coaches should call out commands as the fielder fields the ball. For example, for a right-hander, these commands could be "right-left-field, right-left-throw." Coaches should watch to make sure that players drop down using proper technique, center the ball, funnel it, and then skip and throw. For younger players, we recommend that coaches roll the balls underhand. For older players, only one line should be set up at the shortstop position so that longer throws are made to first base. In addition, this is also a good drill for measuring the arm strength of your players. Balls can also be hit or thrown to the forehand and backhand sides.

Fielding Fly Balls

Judging the flight of a fly ball is the most difficult skill an outfielder needs to learn. When a fly ball is hit, the outfielder must stay focused on the ball at all times. He should run to the ball in a typical sprinting fashion—with the glove down—until he is in position to make the catch. When the outfielder reaches the area where the catch will be made, he should slow down and position himself a few feet behind the spot where the ball will be caught; he should stand with his glove-side foot ahead of the other foot. The outfielder should always get back quickly on a ball hit over his head and should run to a spot that will be farther back than the spot of the catch. The outfielder should call the ball, communicating to teammates by shouting, "Mine!" or "I've got it!" at least twice (he should wait to make this call until the ball is at its highest point). The outfielder should catch the ball in front and on the glove side of his head, using two hands if possible, with the arms almost fully extended (see figure 8.10). As the catch is made, he will cushion the impact by bringing the glove down and in toward the chest.

A good throw from the outfield finishes a strong defensive play. After catching the fly ball, the outfielder executes a crow hop forward to distribute the weight on the back leg (see The Crow Hop). As the player lines up the hip, shoulder, and glove with the target (second base, third base, or home plate), the player's throwing arm extends loosely behind. The player's weight comes forward, and the player pushes hard off the throwing-side leg while releasing the ball from an overhand position. The momentum of the throw brings the back leg off the ground, and the player continues to move forward after the throw. Accurate, low, one-bounce throws are best (see Relays and Cutoffs later in the chapter).

FIGURE 8.10 Catching a fly ball.

COACHING TIP When running after a fly ball, a player should try to have as little head movement as possible. Make sure your outfielders run on the balls of their feet. If they run flat-footed or on their heels, this will make it seem as if the ball is moving up and down as they run, making it more difficult to judge the ball's flight path.

🎾 FIELDING FLY BALLS DRILL

Description

Depending on the number of players on the team, two or three coaches should be used in this drill. Divide players equally into two or three lines. Station a coach about 20 feet in front of and facing the first player in each line (distance can be increased for older players). The first player in line assumes the ready position, and on command, he moves in the direction in which the coach points. The coach can point left, right, or directly over the head of the player (players in line should be spaced so that they do not interfere with the play). The player starts moving in the direction pointed to, and the coach throws or hits a fly ball in that direction. Coaches can observe fielding technique and provide feedback.

Catching Line Drives

A line drive is a hard hit that moves directly in a line lower to the ground, instead of in a gentle arc as a fly ball does. Because it is usually hit harder and lower to the ground, the line drive is more difficult to judge than the lazy fly ball. When a line drive is hit toward an outfielder, the player's first instinct should be to move backward. If the player moves forward because he senses that the ball is on a lower flight path, he will often be fooled and then not be able to get back to the ball if it is actually going to fly over his head. Outfielders should use good running form and sprint to the spot where they think they will meet the ball. Unlike the fly ball, which is caught in a more upright position, the low line drive should be caught in a crouched position. In this position, the player's head will stay more or less even with the ball. Players should catch line drives above the waist with their arm extended and their fingers pointing up, if possible. This way, if a player tries to catch the ball and the ball pops out, the player still has the ability to quickly turn the glove over and get the dropped ball. Not all line drives can be caught above the waist, so an outfielder should be prepared to rotate his wrist and catch the line drive below the waist with the fingers pointing down (see figure 8.11).

FIGURE 8.11 Catching a low line drive.

🏐 LINE DRIVE DRILL

Description

Depending on the number of players on the team, two or three coaches should be used in this drill. Divide players equally into two or three lines. Station a coach about 50 feet in front of and facing the first player in each line (distance can be increased for older players). The first player in line assumes the ready position, and on command, sprints toward the coach. While the player is running toward him, the coach throws (or hits) a line drive at the player. The coach can vary the force and the distance of the throw so that it mimics the various kinds of line drives that a player will have to catch in a game. If the ball is thrown softly, the player may have to run harder or even dive to catch the ball on the fly. If the coach throws the ball with a little more zip, the player may have to slow down so that the ball does not fly over his head. Coaches can also throw slightly left or right of the oncoming player to make the throw act like a curving line drive, forcing the player to react on the run. Throughout this drill, coaches can observe fielding technique and provide feedback.

Defensive Tactical Skills

It is often said that defense is more important than offense. Considering that runs are often scored without the benefit of a hit, it would be difficult to prove that statement false. That's why your players must learn to work together as a team on defense. For example, if players aren't in the right positions according to the situation on the field, or if they fail to coordinate a good relay throw, an opposing baserunner can advance or even score. Once your team understands and can properly execute the individual defensive technical skills, they can begin putting them together into defensive tactics—or strategies—and they can begin to develop their sense of when to use these tactics. Following are the defensive tactics that you should teach your players at the youth levels. *Note:* Leagues at certain levels may not allow all of these tactics; check your league's rule book.

COACHING TIP At younger levels, there's no need for complicated adjustments in defensive positioning because the offensive tactics your opponents are using aren't that complicated, either. For players aged 12 and under, you should stick to the basics, such as moving players slightly in or out or left or right based on the hitter's power and whether he's right- or left-handed.

Positioning

Positioning is a primary tactical concern of any team defense. Coaches need to adjust players' positions on the field according to the type of hitter at bat, the inning and score of the game, the ability of the pitcher, and many other factors.

They may even have to consider the condition of the field. In baseball, positioning isn't as simple as telling your players, "If your opponent does this, you do that." Instead, you'll have to base your positioning instructions on the tactics you've practiced and the strategies that the other team uses.

Following are some of the things that you and your players will want to take into account when determining the best positioning for your team:

- *Batting side.* If the batter is right-handed, the ball will most likely be hit (pulled) to the left side of the field, and the opposite is usually true for left-handers. So, fielders should move left or right a few steps from their normal position according to the batter's hitting side. You should also factor in the skill of your pitcher before deciding how far to tell players to move. If your pitcher is fast, the fielders should not move left or right as much because the batter may swing late on pitches (instead of hitting to his strong side, the batter may hit to the opposite side). Likewise, if the pitcher is not very fast, then fielders may have to take more than two steps to a batter's pull side.

- *Batting tendencies.* Coaches and players should watch an opposing team closely during a game, remember what each batter did his previous times at bat, and then adjust accordingly. If a batter tried to bunt for a hit earlier in a game or in other games, corner infielders should be moved in to guard against the bunt. If a player always pulls the ball, teams should shift to the pull side of the batter.

- *Batter's physical size.* Since there is often great variation in body size in youth leagues, players should also move backward or forward on the field according to the size of the batter. At younger ages, size is a good indicator of strength and estimated power.

- *Baserunning tendencies.* In leagues where stealing is permitted, if the opponent likes to steal bases, the middle infielders should be positioned closer to second base so they can get there more quickly in the event of a steal attempt.

Backup Responsibilities

Inevitably, a few hits and throws will get by your fielders. But it isn't so much the initial mistake that hurts your team, but rather the series of mistakes that follow if your players don't know their backup responsibilities and how to back players up properly.

Every time a ball is hit in a baseball game, every player in the field must move, not just the player to whom the ball is hit. Make sure all players know where to move on any given play. In general, every base should be covered on every play, and each player covering a base should be backed up. For example, if a runner gets trapped between bases and a rundown is about to take place, all players on the team—outfielders included—should move toward the rundown area to provide backup in case of overthrows. Some players should go directly into position to back up the players executing the rundown, while others should move to cover the next base in case there is a bad throw. If backups aren't in place, disasters can occur. Many good sources are available that show coaches where players should be positioned on each play. Two of the more common plays—relays and cutoffs—that require backup are discussed here.

Relays

Sometimes the distance that a throw has to travel is farther than a player is able to throw. When this occurs, the team needs to have a relay system in place. When a fly ball is hit deep to an outfielder, the appropriate infielder runs toward the outfielder and lines up with the base to which the infielder intends to relay the throw. Typically, the shortstop and second-base player are responsible for moving out to receive throws from the outfielders and relaying them to the appropriate base. The shortstop handles all relay throws from the left and center fielders, and the second-base player takes throws from the right fielder (see figure 8.12).

Only one relay person is needed on most throws, but if the ball is hit very deep, a team may need to use two or even three relay players because of the length of the throw. Especially with younger players, coaches should use a relay system that takes into account the possibility of weaker outfield arms. If the outfielder or infielder does not have a strong arm, the relay person will have to get closer to the origin of the throw.

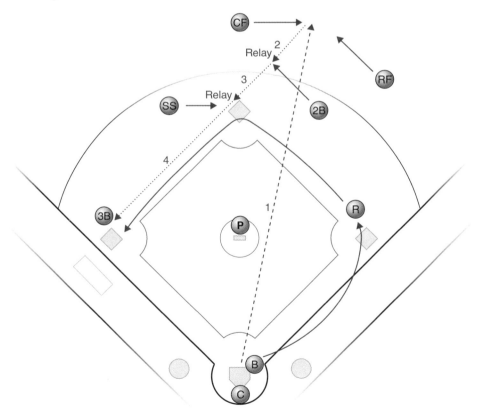

FIGURE 8.12   Relay responsibilities.

Cutoffs

A cutoff is similar to a relay in that a player is stationed between the outfielder and the base to which the throw is made; however, the tactical reason to cut off a throw before it gets to a base is different from a relay throw. A cutoff player gets into a position approximately 25 feet ahead of the base where the play is to be made, between the fielder throwing the ball and that base. The cutoff player serves as an aiming point for the outfielder making the throw. The outfielder should aim to throw the ball at the cutoff player's thighs. If the outfielder's throw is aimed any higher, the chances of it sailing over the head of the cutoff player increase. By aiming lower, the outfielder gives the cutoff player a good chance to field the ball, even if it bounces. If a ball misses the cutoff player, this may allow the baserunner to advance to the next base. The player cutting off the throw catches the ball (unless the player covering the base tells him to let it go through) and either relays the throw to the base or throws to another base to make a play on a trailing runner. Most throws that are cut off are to third base or home plate. The third-base player is the cutoff player on throws from left field to home (see figure 8.13a), and the first-base player is the cutoff on throws from center field and right field to home (see figure 8.13b). The shortstop is the cutoff player for throws to third base (see figure 8.13c). The pitcher backs up these throws either at third or home.

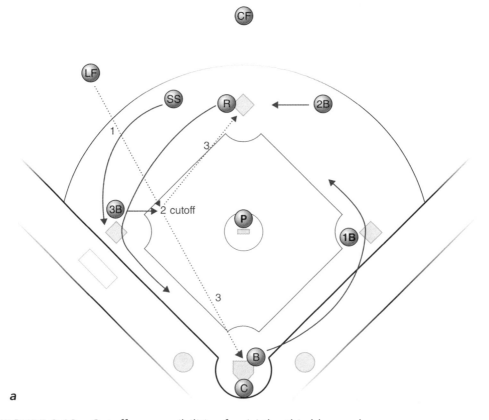

FIGURE 8.13 Cutoff responsibilities for (a) the third-base player.

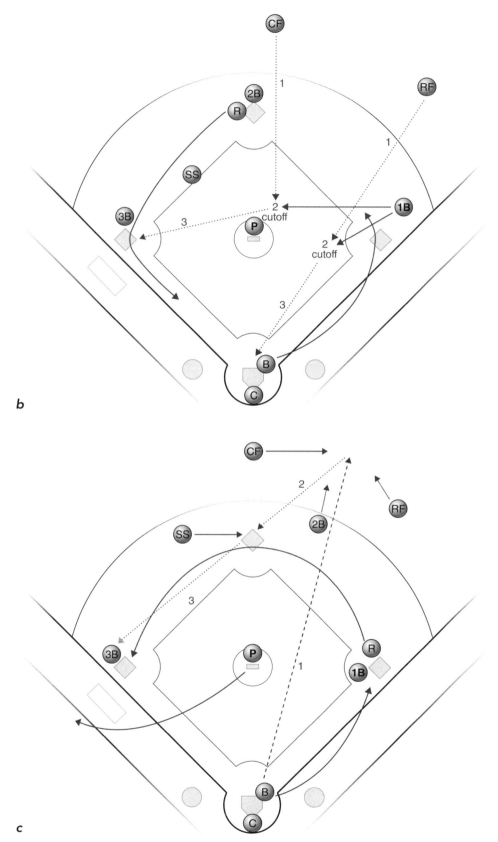

FIGURE 8.13 *(continued)* Cutoff responsibilities for *(b)* the first-base player and *(c)* the shortstop.

☝ HIT THE RELAY

Description

Play on a field appropriate for the age group. Three players participate in this game at a time—one in right field, one at shortstop, and one at third base. The coach hits or throws the ball so the right fielder needs to move to get it. The right fielder must then complete a relay throw toward third base. The shortstop should start at his normal position and then move into position to get the throw from the outfielder. One point is awarded for throws caught in the air by the shortstop. One point is also awarded for relays to third base in which the third-base player catches the ball either straddling the bag or with one foot touching the side of the bag. If the throw is wider than that, no points are awarded. After the three players have scored six points, replace them with three other players and begin again.

Variations

- To make the game easier for younger or less skilled players, hit the ball a shorter distance.
- To make the game more challenging for older or more skilled players, add a runner on first base who attempts to advance to third on the hit.

Special Defensive Plays

The defense controls the ball in baseball, so technically they make the outs in a game, not the batters or runners. Since there are so many ways for a defensive player to get an offensive player out, coaches need to school their teams regularly in the tactics involved in those plays.

Force Plays

A force play occurs when a baserunner must go to the next base on a ground ball because the batter has also become a baserunner (e.g., a batter running to first on a ground ball forces a runner on first to go to second, because you can't have two runners on one base). Runners are not forced to advance to the next base on balls caught in the air. Runners who are forced to advance, however, are put out when the defense gets the ball to the base ahead of the runner. A defensive player must be in possession of the ball and touching the base (typically with a foot, but not necessarily so) before the runner arrives for the runner to be put out.

A force play can be made at all three bases and home plate; the basic techniques are the same, regardless of the base. The player throwing the ball should make the throw chest high to the player covering the base, who should wait for the ball on the side of the base nearest the source of the throw. Once the throw is on the way and the covering player knows where the throw will arrive, the player should step back with the throwing-side foot and place the heel of that foot on the base (as described previously in Covering First Base). The player should stretch out to meet the throw with the glove hand and the glove-side foot. If the throw is slightly off target to one side or the other, the player should step to meet the ball with the foot closest to the ball and should contact the base with the other foot. If the play is going to be close, the player should stretch as far as he can and catch the ball in the glove hand only. If the play is not going to be close, the player should stretch a comfortable distance and catch the ball with both hands.

⚾ LEAD RUNNER

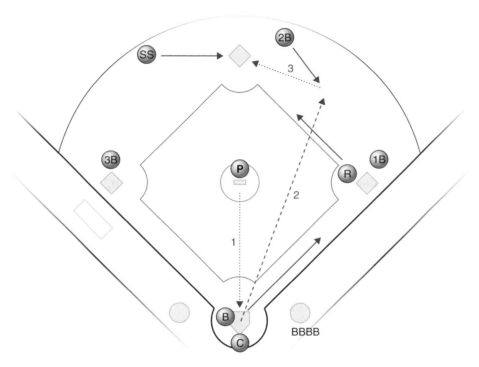

FIGURE 8.14 Lead runner drill.

Description

Play 6v6 on a field appropriate for the age group. For the defense, players are positioned in the infield (first base, second base, shortstop, and third base) and at pitcher and catcher. To begin, one runner is on first and a batter is at the plate, with the remaining offensive players waiting for a turn at bat (see figure 8.14). The pitcher (or coach) throws pitches that are easy to hit, and the batter attempts to hit grounders (the batter hits until he hits a ground ball). The defense tries to make force plays at second. For younger players, the runner cannot leave the base until the ball is hit. Older players should start from a primary lead position but should use judgment and not run until they are forced to. One point is awarded to the defense for every force made at second. Repeat with the next player in line as the batter and the previous batter on first base. After each player has had two turns, the offensive team will become the defensive team, and play continues.

Variations

- To make the game easier for younger or less skilled players, have batters hit off a tee, or the coach can hit or throw the ball to locations that will make the play easier.
- To make the game more challenging for older or more skilled players, shorten the distance between first and second base; allow the runner to take off on the pitch; or the coach can hit or throw the ball to locations that will make the play more difficult.

Tag Plays

A tag-play situation occurs any time a runner is not required to move to the next base but tries to do so at his own risk. To put out a baserunner on a tag play, the defensive player must tag or touch the runner with the ball, or with the glove holding the ball, when the runner is off the base. Tag-play situations typically occur when a runner on second base (with no runner on first base) runs on a ground ball, when a runner on second base attempts to score on a base hit, when a runner tagging up on a fly ball attempts to advance to the next base, or when a runner attempts to steal a base.

The throw for a tag play should arrive just below the knees of the covering player. The runner will probably be sliding into the base, so the throw should be low and close to the runner. This minimizes the time it takes for the covering player to move the glove and ball into position to tag the runner.

More than one technique, however, is acceptable for covering a base on a tag play. The covering player's position at the base depends on the path of the runner and the path of the incoming ball. In general, the player should straddle the base (see figure 8.15a) or stand just to the side of the base facing the direction of the incoming runner (see figure 8.15b). Players should never place a leg between the base and the approaching runner. Instead, they should leave the path to the base open to the runner. With younger players, the recommended method is for the covering player to position himself at the base where he can tag the runner with limited chances of being knocked down or injured. For example, on a tag play at third base, the third-base player could stand in foul territory waiting to receive the ball; this position helps eliminate the risk of a collision.

Covering players should position themselves so that they can catch the ball and bring the gloved ball down to the edge of the base where the runner will arrive. As the runner slides in, the player should let the runner tag himself out by sliding into the gloved ball. The player should then lift the ball out of the way of the runner to avoid losing control of the ball.

FIGURE 8.15   Covering a base for a tag play: *(a)* straddling the base and *(b)* standing to the side of the base.

TAG OUT

Description

Divide the team into two squads of six players each (or adjust according to team size). Play on a field appropriate for the age group, with players at second base, third base, shortstop, and right field for the defensive team. For the offensive team, a runner is on second base, and the rest of the players wait in foul territory to alternate with that runner (each taking turns running). Each play starts with a runner on second (see figure 8.16). The coach hits the ball, alternating between fly-outs to the right fielder in which the runner must tag up and ground balls to second base and shortstop (no balls are hit to third, because the runner wouldn't try to advance in such a situation). On the hit, the runner attempts to advance to third, and the defense tries to get the runner out at third base. One point is awarded to the defense if the runner is tagged out. After two times through the lineup, rotate offense and defense. Also make certain that the two extra defensive players see action.

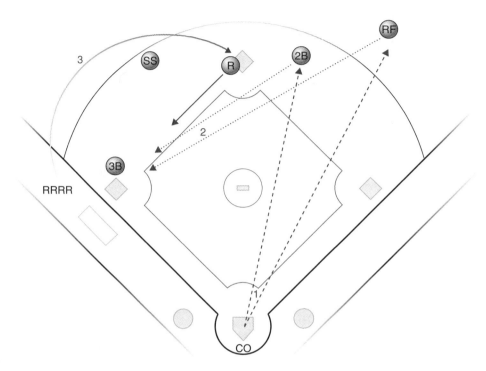

FIGURE 8.16   Tag out drill.

Variations

- To make the game easier for younger or less skilled players, limit hits to the infield and do not use an outfielder, or move the outfielder in closer.
- To make the game more challenging for older or more skilled players, hit the ball to locations that will make the play more difficult.

Double Plays

A double play occurs any time two offensive players are put out during continuous action. Examples include a fly-out in which a baserunner is put out after failing to tag up or is tagged out at the next base after correctly tagging up; a strikeout and a runner thrown out on the same play trying to steal; and a ground ball with a runner on first, with force-outs made at second and first bases. Double plays are rally killers for the offense and morale boosters for the defense.

With less than two outs and a runner (or runners) in a force situation, the first option is usually to cut down the lead runner. Once the lead runner is put out at one base, the covering player at that base throws to first base to complete the double play. Here we'll focus on executing the second-to-first double play.

COACHING TIP Double plays are very difficult to execute, especially with younger players, because more players usually must handle the ball, more throws have to be made, and as a result, more time is used. In addition, younger players play on fields where the distance between bases is shorter. However, as players advance in their skills and begin to play on larger fields—when they reach the 13- to 15-year age group—they can learn to execute double plays.

Ground Balls to the Right Side of Second On ground balls hit to the right side of second base, the shortstop will cover second base (the second-base player may be moving to field the ball). In this situation, the shortstop will use the shortstop drag technique to make the force play. When throws are made by the first- or second-base player from the outfield side of the baseline between first and second base, the shortstop moves just behind second base, straddling the back corner of the bag (the corner pointing to center field) with the inside of the right foot, and faces the thrower (see figure 8.17). If there is no time to straddle the bag, the shortstop moves

FIGURE 8.17 Shortstop drag.

through this position without stopping. As the shortstop catches the ball and makes the force-out, she steps toward the right outfield grass with the left foot (see figure 8.18a), dragging the toes of the right foot across the back corner of the base (see figure 8.18b). She then makes the throw to first base.

FIGURE 8.18 Shortstop drag without a stop.

Balls Fielded by the Pitcher or Catcher   On balls fielded by the pitcher or catcher, the shortstop covers second and uses an inside pivot to make the force-out and complete the throw to first. The shortstop steps on the inside corner of the base with the left foot, facing the player with the ball, and bends his knees as he catches the ball (see figure 8.19a). He then springs off that foot toward the pitcher's mound, landing on the right foot out of the path of the runner (see figure 8.19b). The shortstop then steps toward first and makes the throw (see figure 8.19c).

FIGURE 8.19   Shortstop inside pivot.

Ground Balls to the Left Side of Second   On ground balls hit to the left side of second base, the second-base player covers the base. He uses either a crossover pivot or a rocker pivot.

A crossover pivot is used on any throw from the third-base player and long throws from the shortstop. To execute the crossover pivot, the second-base player approaches second so he can cross the base in a direct line toward the player feeding him the ball. If time allows, he moves to a position just short of the base, facing the thrower. As the ball approaches, the second-base player steps on the base with his left foot, moves over the base, and catches the ball on the far side of the base while still in contact with it (see figure 8.20a). The second-base player stops his forward momentum by landing on the right foot; with this step, he should be out of the base path. He then shifts his weight to the left side by stepping to the left and makes the throw to first base (see figure 8.20b).

FIGURE 8.20 Second-base player crossover pivot.

A rocker pivot is used by the second-base player on short throws from the shortstop. To execute the rocker pivot, the second-base player moves to the base and places the toes of his left foot in contact with the outfield side of the base (see figure 8.21a). With the weight on the left foot as shown in figure 8.21a, he catches the ball, makes the force-out, and steps back onto the right foot (see figure 8.21b). The player then steps left toward first base and throws the ball to first to try to complete the double play (see figure 8.21c).

FIGURE 8.21 Second-base player rocker pivot.

⚾ DOUBLE TROUBLE

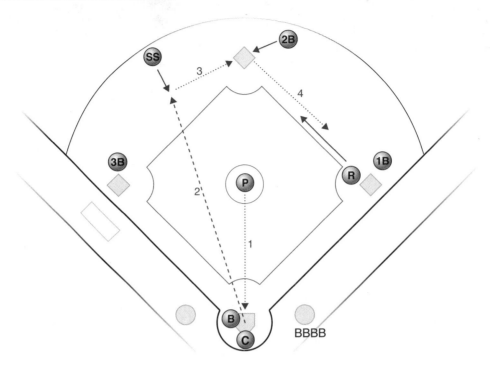

FIGURE 8.22   Double trouble drill.

Description

Play 6v6 on a field appropriate for the age group. For the defense, players are positioned in the infield (first base, second base, shortstop, and third base) and at pitcher and catcher. To begin, one runner is on first and a batter is at the plate, with the remaining offensive players waiting for a turn at bat (see figure 8.22). The pitcher (or coach) throws pitches that are easy to hit, and the batter attempts to hit ground balls (the batter hits until he hits a ground ball). The defense tries to make a double play. For younger players, the runner cannot leave the base until the ball is hit. Older players should start from a primary lead position but should use judgment and not run until they are forced to. One point is awarded to the defense for every force made at second, and two points are awarded if a double play is made. Repeat with the next player in line as the batter and the previous batter on first base. After each player has had two turns, the offensive team will become the defensive team, and play continues.

Variations

- To make the game easier for younger or less skilled players, have batters hit off a tee, or the coach can hit or throw the ball to locations that will make the play easier.

- To make the game more challenging for older or more skilled players, shorten the distance between first and second base, or the coach can hit or throw the ball to locations that will make the play difficult.

Defensive Strategies

Although the old saying about every rule being made to be broken can ring true in baseball, there are several hard-and-fast principles that coaches should instill in their players. These should be constantly drilled and repeated in practices until they become second nature to all players. Following are some of the more crucial defensive principles in the game:

- **Always try to get the lead runner.** The lead runner is the one farthest advanced on the bases. The defense's objective is to stop the player closest to scoring by throwing the ball to the base ahead of the lead runner.

- **Look the runner back.** On ground balls in certain tag-play situations, a fielder can look a runner back to the base before throwing to first for the out, thus keeping the runner from advancing. For example, when a runner is on second and a ground ball is hit to the third-base player, that fielder should field the ball (focusing entirely on fielding it first!), and as he begins the throwing motion, he should look quickly at the runner to freeze the runner. Unless the runner tries to advance, the fielder should not stop or slow the throwing motion. If the runner does try to advance, the fielder is ready to make a play on the runner. If the fielder doesn't pay attention to the runner, the runner will likely be able to advance.

- **Back up the throw.** Every player not directly involved in a play should back up throws to different parts of the field. The pitcher backs up the base that the lead runner is moving toward, especially if it's home plate. Infielders back each other up when a throw is coming from the catcher.

- **Back up the hit.** Outfielders not directly involved in a play back up infielders or each other. If the ball gets away from one outfielder, the backup can make the play and prevent runners from taking an extra base.

- **Give up a run.** Sometimes you'll decide to give up a run in exchange for an out because you have a comfortable lead. In this case, you might let a runner on third score on a ground ball to get the easier out at first.

- **Get the first out.** In a double-play situation, the first out must be the lead runner. If infielders retire the lead runner, they can attempt to complete the double play.

Again, keep your defensive strategies simple and the number of them manageable. Defense requires quick reactions. If you overload players with too much information or your defensive strategies are too difficult, players won't be able to respond quickly and properly when the ball is hit.

Rundowns

Rundown situations occur when a runner is caught between bases by the defense. The two defenders closest to the bases that the runner is caught between are the primary defenders; the two fielders next closest to these bases are backup fielders in the rundown. Backup fielders should stay at least 10 feet behind the primary fielders unless the play has moved close to a base. If a primary fielder throws the ball to a teammate, the player who threw the ball becomes a backup fielder, and the player backing him up assumes a primary fielding role. When one runner is in a rundown and another runner is on third base, the defense needs to keep a close watch on the runner on third, who may try to score. Fielders must be ready to throw the ball home to cut down the runner trying to score.

To execute a rundown, the fielder with the ball initiates the play by holding the ball up, ready to throw, and running directly at the baserunner until the runner commits to moving toward one base or the other. The fielder awaiting the ball at a base should not wait on the base, but should be positioned a few steps ahead of the base to cut down the distance of the rundown. If the first fielder can't make the tag, the ball is thrown to the player whom the runner is going toward. Ideally, the runner should be forced to run back to the last base occupied, rather than forward to the next base—for example, a runner caught between third base and home should be forced to run back toward third—but the main goal of a rundown is to get the runner out no matter where that is. On a rundown, fielders should try to get the runner out with one throw. Two throws may be okay, but more than two is too many, opening the gate for errors or for other runners advancing. The throw should be by the side of the runner, rather than over the runner's head. Fielders should tag the runner with the ball in their glove, not just held in their hand; in fact, it's preferable to use the bare hand to cover the ball in the glove to make sure it's secure. Once the fielder has made a throw, he must get out of the baseline so he doesn't obstruct the runner if the runner reverses directions.

☉ PICKLE

Description

Set up four stations, each with two bases positioned approximately 30 feet apart; one base is designated as second base and the other as third. Three players will play at each station—two fielders and one runner. The runner starts about 10 feet from one of the bases. The ball is in the hand of the fielder closest to the runner. On the coach's command, a rundown begins, and the runner tries to reach a base safely. Three points are awarded to each of the defensive players for getting the runner out with one throw, two points for getting the runner out with two throws, one point for getting the runner out with three throws, and no points for getting the runner out with four or more throws. If the runner reaches one of the bases safely, he gets six points. Play is completed when the runner is either safe or out. After each rundown ends, players switch positions (the fielders take turns being runners) and restart with the runner again 10 feet from one of the bases. Play ends when each player has taken three turns running.

Variations

- To make the game easier for younger or less skilled players, allow the fielders to get the runner out with any number of throws.
- To make the game more challenging for older or more skilled players, require the runner to be thrown out in two or fewer throws, or add another fielder at each of the bases.

🎾 MAKING THE PLAY

Description

Play 6v6 on a field appropriate for the age group. For the defense, players are positioned in the infield (first base, second base, shortstop, and third base) and at pitcher and catcher. Offensive players are runners; they rotate in as specified for each play. The procedure for each play is as follows:

- *Throws to first.* The coach hits one ground ball to each fielder (including a bunt for the catcher). Each fielder must field the ball and make a throw to first. On contact, a runner stationed in the batter's box runs to first and tries to beat the throw. On the ball hit to the first-base player, the pitcher must cover first. Award one point to the defense for each out.
- *Throws to second.* The coach hits one ground ball to each fielder (including a bunt for the catcher). Each fielder must field the ball and throw to second. On contact, a runner at first runs to second from a leadoff position and tries to beat the throw. Younger players must be stationed on the base until the ball is hit. Award one point to the defense for each out.
- *Throws to home.* The coach hits one ground ball to each infielder (except the catcher). Each fielder must field the ball and throw home. A runner at third runs home on contact and tries to beat the throw. Award one point to the defense for each out.

Rotate offense and defense after the three sets of plays are executed.

Variations

- To make the game easier for younger or less skilled players, hit easy grounders directly to the players.
- To make the game more challenging for older or more skilled players, hit balls randomly to fielders instead of in sequence, hit harder ground balls, or hit ground balls that force the fielders to move in one direction or another.

🎾 AIRTIGHT D

Description

Play 5v5 on a field appropriate for the age group, with a pitcher and players at first, second, third, and shortstop for the defensive team. Offensive players are runners; they rotate in as specified for each play. The procedure for each play is as follows:

- *No runners on base.* A runner is in the batter's box, ready to run to first. The coach, stationed safely away from the runner, hits a ground ball to a fielder (any fielder the coach chooses), without telling the fielders where the ball will be hit. The fielder tries to throw the runner out at first.

- *Runner on first.* A runner is on first base, and a runner is at home, ready to run to first. The coach hits a ground ball to a fielder, who makes the appropriate play (preferably to second base to get the lead runner, but depending on the hit, the throw might need to go to first base).

- *Runner on second.* A runner is on second, and a runner is at home, ready to run to first. The coach hits a ground ball to a fielder, who attempts to hold the runner at second and throw the runner out at first (or throw the runner out at third if he attempts to go).

- *Runner on third.* A runner is on third, and a runner is at home, ready to run to first. Infield is in for the play at the plate. The coach hits a ground ball to a fielder, who must make the appropriate play—throwing home to get the runner or holding the runner at third and throwing to first (or throwing to first if there is no chance to get the runner going home).

Repeat plays three times with the same defense in the field, alternating hits so that all players have about an equal amount of plays to make. Award one point to the defense for every out recorded—unless you judge that the fielder should have tried for an out at second, third, or home rather than throwing to first. After three cycles, rotate offense and defense.

Variations

- To make the game easier for younger or less skilled players, use fewer cycles, use no baserunners, or merely call out the play.

- To make the game more difficult for older or more skilled players, hit challenging ground balls to the fielders.

🎾 ON THE FLY

Description

Play 6v6 on a field appropriate for the age group, with three outfielders, two infielders (for plays to right field, use a second-base player; for plays to center or left, use a shortstop), and a catcher for the defensive team. Offensive players are runners; they rotate in as specified for each play. The coach alternates hitting (or throwing) fly balls to the three outfielders. On each play, the runner or runners advance at their own risk based on the game situation. The outfielders must catch the ball and make the appropriate play in each of these situations:

- A runner is on first, no outs. Infielders are at second and shortstop.
- A runner is on second, no outs. Infielders are at second or shortstop and third.
- A runner is on third, no outs. Infielders are at second or shortstop and third.
- Runners are on first and second, no outs. Infielders are at second or shortstop and third.
- Runners are on second and third, no outs. Infielders are at second or shortstop and third.

Award one point to the defense for every out—whether by fly balls caught or baserunners put out. Subtract one point from the defense if one or more baserunners advance on the play. Rotate offense and defense after each outfielder has had five catchable fly balls.

Variations

- To make the game easier for younger or less skilled players, throw or hit shallower fly balls, or throw or hit fly balls directly at the outfielders.
- To make the game more challenging for older or more skilled players, hit deeper fly balls, or hit balls in the gaps or in front of the outfielders.

SQUEEZE PLAY

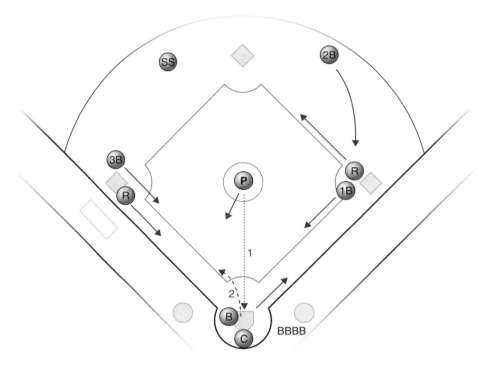

FIGURE 8.23 Squeeze play drill.

Description

Divide the squad in half. Play 6v6 on a field appropriate for the age group, with defensive players positioned in the infield (first base, second base, shortstop, and third base) and at pitcher and catcher. To begin, runners are placed on first and third base, and a batter is at the plate, with the remaining offensive players on the sideline awaiting their turn at bat (see figure 8.23). The pitcher throws pitches that are easy to hit, and the batter attempts to bunt the ball. On each pitch, the runner at third base reacts as if the bunt were a safety squeeze bunt and attempts to score, while the runner at first reacts as if it were a normal sacrifice bunt. The defense attempts to throw the runner out at home plate, force the runner at second base, or get the bunter running to first. Three points are awarded to the defense if the runner is out at home, two points if the runner is out at second, and one point if the batter is out at first. At the conclusion of each play, the runner who began on first base moves to third base and begins the next play as the runner there. Rotate offense and defense after each player on the offensive team has had a turn at bat.

Variations

*   To make the game easier for younger or less skilled players, place a runner on first base only (or keep runners on first and third, but the runner on third doesn't have to try to score).

*   To make the game more challenging for older or more skilled players, make the runner on third react as if the bunt were a suicide squeeze.

This chapter focuses on the offensive techniques and tactics that players need to learn in order to perform effectively in youth baseball games. Remember to use the IDEA approach to teaching skills: introduce, demonstrate, and explain the skill, and attend to players as they practice the skill (see chapter 6). This chapter also ties directly into the season and practice plans in chapter 11, describing the technical skills and team tactics that you'll teach at the practices outlined there. If you aren't familiar with baseball skills, you may find it helpful to watch a video so you can see the skills performed correctly.

The information in this book is limited to baseball basics. As your players advance in their skills, you will need to advance your knowledge as a coach. You can do this by learning from your experiences, watching and talking with more experienced coaches, and studying resources on advanced skills.

Offensive Technical Skills

The offensive technical skills you will teach your players include hitting and baserunning. Mastering these skills will allow your players to better execute your offensive tactics—or strategies—during the game. These basic technical skills serve as the foundation for playing baseball well at all levels. Baseball players practice these techniques at every practice, from youth baseball to the pros.

Hitting

Even though it may be difficult, hitting a baseball is one of the most satisfying things to do in sports. The feeling of solid contact as the bat connects with the ball is a sensation that is unsurpassed. But hitting is a skill that must be developed through constant practice and coaching. Good hitters perform the skill in one fluid motion. However, there are four separate components to hitting that should be taught to young players: grip, stance, stride, and swing.

COACHING TIP To gain better bat control and speed, younger players should choke up on the bat so the bottom of the lower hand (the left hand for a right-handed batter) is about two inches above the knob of the bat. Older players can use this trick as well, especially when they are facing a very fast pitcher and they need to increase their bat speed.

Grip

Players should grip a bat with their dominant hand positioned above the less dominant one. A right-handed batter would place his left hand closest to the knob of the bat and place his right hand above the left hand, whereas a left-handed batter would do the opposite. The batter should grip the bat with his fingers, not with the palms of his hands. The middle knuckles (the knuckles that a person knocks on a door with) of each hand should be lined up with each other (see figure 9.1). This hand alignment reduces tension. Because tightened muscles make a swing slower, players should hold the bat loosely until they are ready to make the swing; at that point, their grip will automatically tighten as they move the bat forward to meet the ball (see Swing for more information).

FIGURE 9.1 Proper grip on the bat.

Stance

When at bat, your players need to be comfortable in the batter's box. A stance that feels good to one player may feel awkward to another. You don't need to force every batter to assume the same stance at the plate. However, you should stress that batters need to position themselves in a square stance with the feet comfortably wider than shoulder-width apart (as shown in figure 9.2). The player should stand back from the plate far enough so the bat passes slightly across the outer edge of the plate when the player's arms are fully extended on the swing. The back foot should be parallel to the back line of the batter's box, and the front foot should be parallel to the front line of the box, toes pointing toward the plate. The knees will be slightly bent, with the player's weight centered on the balls of the feet and distributed approximately 60 percent over the back foot and 40 percent over the front. The player's upper body

FIGURE 9.2 Proper stance at the plate.

should be bent slightly at the waist, and the bat should be held at a 45-degree angle to the ground. The player's elbows should be out from the body and flexed, pointing down toward the ground.

Stride and Coil

To properly hit a baseball, a hitter must shift his weight toward the backside (this shift back is called the *coil*) and then shift it forward again before swinging the bat. This movement helps the player generate momentum and a quicker swing.

For most hitters, however, this forward shift is preceded by a short step toward the pitcher with the front foot. This step is called the *stride*. A hitter doesn't need to stride to hit, but if a player does take a stride, he needs to make sure that the step is small and that he takes his stride before contact, not at contact.

If a player takes a stride, the player should begin to rotate the front shoulder, hip, and knee slightly inward when the pitcher's hand is about to release the ball. The slight rotation of these body parts causes the hands to move three or four inches backward and shifts most of the hitter's weight toward the back foot. When the pitcher releases the ball, the hitter should take a short step forward (the stride) with his front foot, being careful not to shift his weight forward while doing so (see figure 9.3*a*). When the stride is complete, most of the player's weight should still be on the inside part of the back foot, and the hands should be cocked in a trigger position just off the back shoulder (see figure 9.3*b*).

The player should be careful not to bring all of the weight forward in the stride because such a premature weight shift will cause the player's head to

FIGURE 9.3 Proper body positioning for the stride.

move forward, creating a loss of momentum and a slower swing. Also, if the hitter takes too big a step forward, called overstriding or lunging at the ball, you should teach the player to widen his stance and reduce or eliminate the stride entirely. Cutting out the stride movement often helps a player keep his weight back longer before the swing.

COACHING TIP A hitter must shift his eyes from a general focus on the pitcher while in the batting stance to a sharp focus on the ball as the pitch is released. For players to accurately judge if a pitch is going to be a ball or a strike, they must be able to track the ball from the pitcher's release to the plate. To help players with this skill, take four baseballs and draw red, black, blue, or green circles on four sides (one color on each ball). One at a time, pitch a ball to each hitter and have the hitter call out the color on the ball.

Swing

Once the player makes the decision to try to hit the pitch, he can begin the swing, which is initiated by the hands, legs, and hips. The hands begin to move toward the ball, the back hip begins to turn, and the player's back foot pivots, lifting the heel off the ground and causing the knee to rotate (see figure 9.4). This rotation of the back side of the body causes the weight to shift forward. At the same time, the front foot remains straight and firm, the front shoulder opens, and the hands come down and move toward the ball, with the lead elbow pointed toward the ground. The barrel of the bat should be parallel to the ground as it moves through the hitting zone, and the hitter should keep the barrel level with or above the hands during the swing. The player should also strive to keep his head upright and still in order to keep an eye on the ball. He should bury his chin in the back shoulder as he finishes the swing.

FIGURE 9.4 Proper positioning for the swing.

Bunting Techniques

When your team has a runner on first or runners on first and second base, a bunt can be used to successfully advance the runners into scoring position. Bunting can also be a good surprise strategy used solely to get on base. The bunt is a good tactic for your players to use against overpowering pitchers and pitchers who end up in a poor fielding position on the follow-through. See Offensive Tactical Skills for more information on the tactical aspects of bunting.

There are two approaches to bunting: the square around method and the pivot method. In the square around method, as the pitcher starts the windup, the batter squares his body toward the pitcher by moving the front foot back a bit and moving the back foot up so that the feet are nearly parallel; in this position, the batter's chest is facing, or square to, the pitcher's mound (see figure 9.5a). In the pivot method, the player simply turns on the balls of both feet at the same time without lifting them; when fully pivoted, both feet are pointed at the pitcher's mound (see figure 9.5b).

FIGURE 9.5 The (a) square around and (b) pivot approaches to bunting.

In both the square around and pivot methods, the knees bend so that the player's weight is forward. This helps prevent the batter from lunging. The player's upper hand slides about a foot toward the barrel of the bat, gripping lightly while keeping the fingers underneath and the thumb on top in the form of a V (see figure 9.6). The bottom hand stays on the handle, and the batter uses the handle to steer the ball in the direction he wants the bunt to go. Ideally, the player places the bunt down the third-base line, so for a right-handed batter, the player must bring the handle close to the body with the bottom hand. To bunt down the first-base line, a right-handed batter must push out the handle toward first base with the bottom hand. The player should not swing the bat, but instead should let the ball come to it. He should "give" with the arms and hands as the bat meets the ball, as if he were catching the ball in a glove.

FIGURE 9.6 Proper hand positioning for a bunt.

FOUR-COUNT HITTING DRILL

Description

Divide players into lines of four or five players each. Lines should be far enough apart from each other that when the players perform the swinging motion, there is no chance that they could hit one another. For younger age groups or less skilled players, we recommend that players do not use bats when performing this drill until they gain proficiency.

To begin the drill, the coach stands in front of the players and acts as the pitcher. The coach calls out specific positions within the batting motion, and the players assume the positions and freeze. Coaches can use the words describing the segment of the batting motion or simply call out numbers that refer to the various segments:

- *Stance or 1:* Players assume a balanced batting stance, with their weight positioned evenly over the feet.
- *Coil or 2:* Players coil by rotating their front shoulders, their front hip, and their front knee backward slightly.
- *Stride or 3:* Players stride forward slightly with their front foot, taking care that their weight does not move forward when the foot strides.
- *Swing or 4:* Players swing toward an imaginary pitch and perform the proper weight shift, head movement, hip turn, and so on. For older or more skilled players, the coach can call out a specific type of pitch (low and outside, for example) and evaluate how the players react.

Baserunning

In baseball, the last thing a team wants to do on the bases is to waste precious scoring opportunities. As a coach, you must teach your players to become heads-up, aggressive baserunners who always know where the ball is, how many outs there are, and what they will do when the ball is hit.

Before you can teach players how to run the bases, however, they first must know the basic mechanics of running. To sprint properly, players need to run on their toes, with a high knee lift and with their arms pumping front to back, not across the body (see figure 9.7). The player's body should lean forward, and the head should be up.

FIGURE 9.7   Proper form for running.

Running to First Base

When a hitter makes contact, he should drop the bat at the end of the swing, then move quickly and efficiently out of the batter's box. The player turns in the direction of first base, stays low, and drives out of the box. A right-handed hitter will start down the line with a jab step of the back foot. A left-handed hitter would start down the line by crossing his left leg over his right foot. The run to first base should be an all-out sprint, and the player should run through the bag, like a sprinter hitting a finish-line tape. Tell your players not to lunge or jump at the bag because this is not as fast as a running step. Also make sure your players are ready to advance to second if the throw to first is inaccurate or is missed. When making the turn to go to second, a player should sprint about a third of the distance to second base and should listen for the first-base coach's commands on whether to go on to second or return to first.

If the player's hit is into the outfield, he should "think second" by running a flat arc to first base and continuing hard past the bag, looking for the opportunity to advance (see Running the Bases for more information on the flat arc). The first-base coach will tell the runner to continue running full speed to second if the outfielder misses the ball or bobbles it. If the outfielder makes a clean stop, the first-base coach will tell the runner to turn and look, which means the runner should make the turn to second, sprint about one-third of the distance to second base, and listen for the first-base coach's commands on whether to go on to second or return to first.

Running the Bases

Runners need to approach each base correctly to maintain momentum and minimize abrupt angles that slow them down. On a base hit to the outfield, the runner begins the flat arc about six feet out of the batter's box (see figure 9.8), curving no more than three feet outside the line. Ideally, runners should hit the left inside corner of the base with the left foot while leaning the left shoulder toward the infield for tight cornering. However, the most important thing is to hit the inside corner at full speed with the foot pointed at the next base. Baserunners should continue the pattern of running flat arcs, hitting the inside corner of the base, and leaning the left shoulder toward the infield any time they anticipate running multiple bases. The first- and third-base coaches will instruct runners on whether to advance, depending on the defensive response to the hit. The base coach will indicate whether to touch the base and move to the next one without hesitation, stop on the base and not attempt to advance because the throw is coming ("On the bag!"), or turn and run about one-third of the way to the next base before stopping ("Turn and look!").

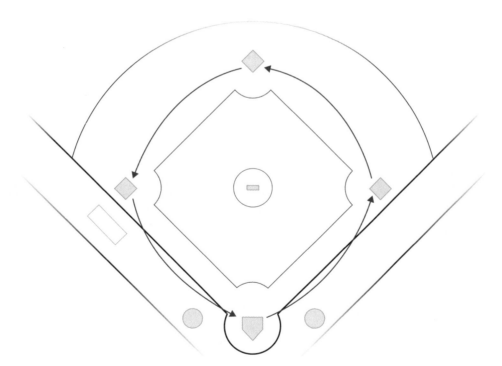

FIGURE 9.8   The flat arc is the most efficient path for rounding the bases.

COACHING TIP Instruct your players to always run all out to first base, regardless of the type of hit. Players should never jog down to first in disgust over a slow ground ball back to the pitcher or a weak pop-up. In addition to presenting themselves as poor sports, players who don't run to first lose the chance to take advantage of an error to get on base. At the younger levels, you just never know when a player might bobble a ball or make a wild throw.

Taking Leadoffs

Once on base, players should know how to take a leadoff—if allowed by league rules—so that they can be in a good position to get to the next base if the batter hits the ball or if the coach calls a steal. A leadoff, typically called the primary lead, is the distance the player takes (usually two or three shuffle steps) toward the next base from the base she is occupying. This primary lead, which will vary from player to player based on the player's quickness and reactions, is most effective because it puts the runner a maximum distance from the base but in a good position to get back to the base if the catcher or pitcher attempts a pickoff.

A player should not take her leadoff until the pitcher has contacted the rubber and is ready to take his sign from the catcher. To initiate movement, the runner takes a short step with the right foot in a direct line to the next base (see figure 9.9a). Keeping the shoulders square to the infield, the player then slides or shuffles the left leg toward the right leg until she gets to a maximum, yet safe, distance from the bag (see figure 9.9b). When shuffling, the player should not bring her feet together in the movement, because this destroys balance and makes it more difficult for the player to return to the base if a pickoff attempt occurs. To stop the movement, the player comes down with the knees slightly bent and in a balanced position with the weight in the center of the body (see figure 9.9c). If

FIGURE 9.9 Taking a leadoff.

a steal has been called, when the pitcher's body motion indicates the start of the pitch, the runner, who is now in the leadoff position, will take a quick crossover step to initiate the attempted steal. Getting this split-second jump on the pitcher is often the difference between being out or safe at the next base.

LEADOFF AND STEAL DRILL

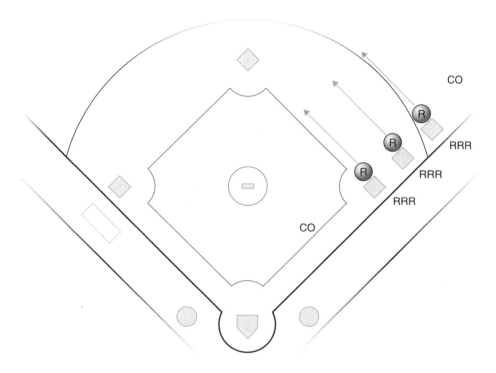

FIGURE 9.10 Leadoff and steal drill.

Description

Place two practice bases along the first-base foul line, with one practice base positioned five feet from first base and the other five feet from the first. Divide players so that there is an equal number at each base and all players are standing in single-file lines in foul territory (see figure 9.10). The coach stands in a position where the players' techniques can be clearly observed. The first player in each line steps forward and occupies the base. On the coach's command, the players take their leadoff from the base, assume the controlled leadoff stance, and then break for second base as if on a steal or a hit. Coaches can observe if players are getting into a controlled, balanced position on the leadoff and whether they are getting too far off the base. Coaches can also watch the players' running form when they break for the base.

Sliding

When approaching a base, a player must decide in an instant whether or not he will need to slide. Typically, if the play at the base appears close or if a coach or teammate is yelling to get down, the player should slide. At the youth level, the bent-leg slide is the most common type of slide used. As a coach, you will need to teach your players how to perform the bent-leg slide safely and correctly, giving them plenty of opportunities to practice it so they become comfortable with the technique.

COACHING TIP   Once a player has made the decision to slide, the player should carry out the slide. Players often get into the habit of changing their minds at the last second, increasing their chances of injury.

The player should begin her slide when she is approximately 10 to 12 feet from the bag. The player shouldn't just drop down to the ground; she should slide to the bag. As the player approaches the bag, she will bend her knees as if she were going to sit in a chair. This movement drops the hips to the ground (see figure 9.11*a*). As she is "sitting down," she will extend her right or left leg toward the bag and bend the other leg under the extended knee to form a "4" shape. The player should slide on her buttocks, not on her side or hips. She should tuck her chin to her chest in order to keep her head up and prevent it from moving backward and hitting the ground. The player's hands should be up; they should not be dragged across the ground as the slide is executed (see figure 9.11*b*). As the player slides to the base, the player's extended foot should be 6 to 8 inches off the ground, as shown in figure 9.11*a*, so that her shoes don't catch the ground and perhaps cause injury.

FIGURE 9.11   Sliding to the base.

OUTFIELD SLIDING DRILL

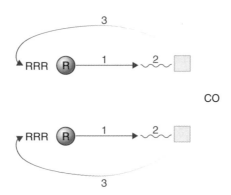

FIGURE 9.12   Outfield sliding drill.

Description

Place two gloves or bases in a soft, grassy area of the outfield. Divide your players into two equal lines about 40 feet away from the gloves or bases (see figure 9.12). The players should remove their shoes. On your command, the first player in each line sprints toward the base opposite their line. When the players get 10 to 12 feet away from the base, you should yell, "Hit it!" On that command, the players execute their slide according to the techniques you have been teaching.

The chance of a player being injured while doing this drill is minimal. Because they are not wearing shoes, they will not catch their feet on the ground accidentally. Also, the outfield grass is much more slippery than infield dirt, so the players will slide more smoothly.

Tagging Up

When a ball is hit in the air, the runner must decide whether to go halfway to the next base or to tag up. *Tagging up* means that the runner remains in contact with the base during the fly ball, with the intention of advancing to the next base after the ball is caught.

Outfield flies are tougher, requiring a quick assessment of how deep the ball is hit, the positioning of the outfield, and the throwing arm of the outfielder who is likely to make the catch. The first- or third-base coach can help make the call. Tell your runners that, in most situations, they should play it safe and not try to advance unless a base coach tells them to do so (though it doesn't hurt to force a difficult throw to the next base by bluffing a run; the hurried throw could be off line). If a runner is going to tag up, he needs to stay low, keep the knees bent, and push hard off the bag on the coach's command to "Go!"

⚾ TAG AND GO DRILL

Description

Several players are in the outfield, and the remaining players stand in a line in foul territory near third base. The first player in line acts as a runner and positions himself about six feet up the line from third base toward home. The coach throws a fly ball to one of the players stationed in the outfield; when the ball is in the air, the runner gets back to the base and assumes the tag-up position. When the ball is caught, the runner tags up and sprints to home plate. Repeat until each runner has had several opportunities. The players in the outfield should then switch with the runners so that everyone gets a chance to tag up.

Offensive Tactical Skills

Once your team understands and can properly execute the individual offensive technical skills, they can begin putting them together into offensive tactics—or strategies—and they can begin to develop their sense of when to use these tactics. Following are the offensive tactics that you should teach your players at the youth levels. *Note:* Leagues at certain levels may not allow all of these tactics; check your league's rule book.

Hitting Strategy

The batter, more than any other offensive player, dictates your team's offensive strategy. You will more likely tell baserunners to run with the pitch if you have a good contact hitter at the plate who has limited power than if there is a power hitter up who strikes out a lot. Why? First, because you know that the contact hitter will probably get the bat on the ball, preventing the possibility of a runner becoming an easy target for a strong-armed catcher on a missed swing by the hitter. Second, a batted ball hit by the contact hitter often won't make it out of the infield. If the lead runner is not running on the pitch, this makes it easier for the defense to get a force-out. And because the power hitter is likely to get the ball beyond the infield if contact is made, there is not a big advantage to sending the runner, because a force-out is unlikely in that case.

A coach should teach players the following things in order to help them gain a tactical advantage when they are at bat:

- Observe the pitcher during warm-ups and on pitches to teammates who bat earlier in the lineup. Ask teammates for information about the speed, location, and type of pitches thrown.

- Once in the batter's box, be aware of the count, the number of outs, and the coach's signal. A missed sign can result in an easy double play. In contrast, a sign that is received and executed can be the start of a big inning. The team should review all signs and signals regularly during practices, and a coach should take time to correct players when a sign is misinterpreted so that it doesn't happen in a game.

- Be willing to accept the fact that outs are part of the game. Even at the professional level, players who hit .300 (the standard of good hitting) make an out 7 out of 10 times.

- Be confident—a good hitter is a confident one. A player can boost his own hitting confidence by staying positive. A player should have the frame of mind that each pitch will be a strike and that he should be ready to swing on every pitch. If he's hoping for a walk because he doubts his ability to get the bat on the ball, then he will not become a successful hitter. A hitter should think *swing*, not *take*!

If your batters are confident at the plate and have acquired the necessary knowledge of tactics during practice, then your team might be ready to apply some of baseball's common offensive strategies during games. Following are some common strategies used at the youth level.

⟲ HITTING DOWN

Description

Play 4v4 on a field appropriate for the age group, with players at first base, second base, third base, and shortstop for the defensive team. To begin, one runner is on first and a batter is at the plate, with the remaining offensive players waiting for a turn at bat. A batting tee is placed at home plate, and the batter must hit a ground ball (the batter hits until he hits a ground ball). The defense attempts to force the runner out at second base or get a double play. If the ball is hit on the ground between fielders and into the outfield, two points are awarded to the offense; one point is awarded if the runner is safe at second base and another point if the runner is safe at first base. Deduct a point for every ball hit into the air. Rotate offense and defense after each player on the offensive team has had a turn at bat. A low line drive should be considered a ground ball for this game.

Variations

- To make the game easier for younger or less skilled players, have no runners on base and award the offense a point if the batter-runner is safe at first.

- To make the game more challenging for older or more skilled players, use live pitching.

Hit-and-Run

A hit-and-run is a play in which a baserunner breaks for the next base as the pitch is thrown and the batter tries to make contact with the ball if the pitch is thrown in the strike zone. Ideally, the batter should try to hit the ball on the ground to the right-field side of the diamond to help break up double-play possibilities and move runners into scoring position. On a hit-and-run, the middle infielders typically react to the breaking runner as if a steal is on and move toward second base, often finding themselves out of position to make a

Communicating With Signs

As a coach, you will need to develop a simple system of hand signals to set plays in motion. Typically, the sign for the play that you are calling is embedded in or tagged onto the end of a series of decoy signals; this helps disguise the play from the other team. Signs can be given in many ways, but overall, coaches should always consider the age and experience level of their players and not make their signs too difficult to see or interpret. Some simple methods you might use include having different body parts stand for different signs—head, steal; chest, bunt; and so on—or using the number of touches to a body part to indicate a sign—touching the belt twice, bunt; touching the cap twice, steal; and so on. You could even use an indicator before a set of signs to signify that a sign will be coming. An example of a simple indicator would be touching the brim of the cap first or grabbing the ear. Indicators can be changed easily on the bench if you think the opponents may be stealing signs. However, don't overload your players with too many signals because they will not be able to execute what they don't understand. If you see that players are having trouble grasping the sign for a specific play or remembering a signal, you may want to simplify or drop it.

Teach your players to watch the entire series of signs, instead of picking up a sign and turning immediately to the batter's box, because you may still be giving additional decoy signs. In addition, instruct your players to react to situations that allow them to take advantage of the defense, even when you haven't called a specific play. For example, if a catcher loses control of a pitch, your baserunners should be ready to take the next base without your telling them to do so.

Here are a few sample hitting and baserunning signals you might use in youth baseball.

	Sign	Message
To batters	Right hand across chest	Swing away
	Right hand to nose	Take pitch
	Right hand to belt	Bunt
	Right hand to ear	Hit-and-run
To baserunners	Left hand to right sleeve	Steal
	Left hand to bill of cap	Delayed steal
	Left hand pointing	Double steal
	Left hand to ear	Hit-and-run
	Left hand patting top of cap	Stay unless a wild pitch, passed ball, or hit
	Left hand across chest	Go on contact
To all	Rubbing hands together	Wipe-off (cancel)
	Right hand pointing	Indicator signal

good fielding play on the batted ball. Even if the ball is hit on the ground and fielded by the second-base player, it will be fielded too late to make a play on the runner, and the fielder will be forced to make a play on the batter running to first. This effectively moves the runner to second base, where it will be easier for him to score on a base hit. If the batted ball gets through the infield, the runner should be able to reach third base—even better scoring position. Your team should not use this strategy if the opposing pitcher is wild (thus making it difficult for the batter to make contact) or if the hitter is not skilled enough to make frequent contact.

HIT-AND-RUN

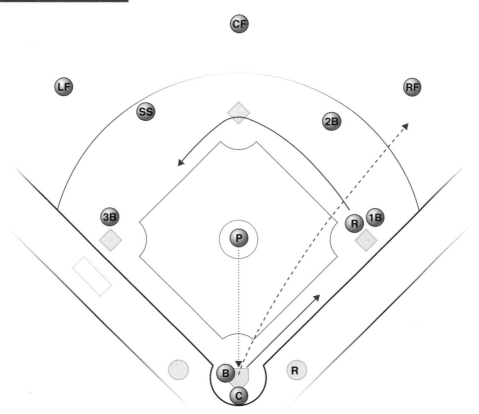

FIGURE 9.13   Hit-and-run drill.

Description

Play 3v9 on a field appropriate for the age group, with an entire defensive team set up in the field. For the offensive team, a batter is at the plate, a runner is on first base, and the remaining player is waiting in the on-deck area (see figure 9.13). The pitcher (or the coach) throws pitches that are easy to hit, and the batter attempts to hit to right field to move the runner up. On the hit, the runner should advance as far as possible without being thrown out. Two points are awarded for a hit that advances a runner to third or home, one point for a hit that advances a runner only to second. No points are awarded for plays that do not advance the runner. Each set of three offensive players gets two at-bats each; after two at-bats, the three players go on defense, and three of the defensive players rotate in to hit.

Variations

- To make the game easier for younger or less skilled players, have batters hit off a tee, or move the outfielders back, making it less difficult for runners to go from first to third.

- To make the game more challenging for older or more skilled players, pitch harder pitches or move the outfielders in.

Bunting

Being able to execute bunts in specific game situations makes your team stronger and more difficult to defend against. Laying down a bunt, especially when the element of surprise is involved, makes the defense move and react quickly. And because the bunt forces the defense to hurry, the chances of advancing a runner or placing an additional runner on base increase greatly for your team. The bunt is also a highly motivational tool because when executed properly it fires up your players and gives them an edge.

A sacrifice bunt is a type of bunt used when the batter's sole responsibility is to advance a baserunner successfully. The batter must focus on placing the ball on a portion of the infield where making a play on the baserunner becomes difficult. The batter must accept that he will most likely be thrown out at first, but the lead runner will be one base closer to home. This play should be used in close ball games when you need to advance a runner and the batter is not a particularly good hitter. It can also be used when your team has a lead in late innings and you want to get an insurance run.

A player may also bunt for the purpose of getting a hit. When bunting for a hit, the main difference from the sacrifice bunt is that the batter waits longer to change from a hitting stance into a bunting stance. The batter should wait until the pitcher is about to release the ball before moving into a bunting stance. This strategy is best used if the first- or third-base player is playing deep and the batter is adept at placing bunts and is also fast enough to beat them out. Bunting for a hit is very effective against slow corner infielders or pitchers who do not react well and do not transition into a good fielding position to cover the territory in front of home plate. When facing a good pitcher, this may be a good option to get a runner on base and put pressure on the defense.

Sacrifice Fly

A sacrifice fly is a play in which a batter hits a fly ball and the baserunner from third tags up and advances home for a score. More often than not, a sacrifice fly just happens in the course of trying for a hit, rather than being a planned strategy. But if the batter is a player who naturally hits many fly balls, the coach may want to alert the runner to be sure to tag up. Young hitters will have great difficulty hitting sacrifice flies intentionally, and you should discourage hitters from trying to do it if you think it may cause them to drop their back shoulder and swing with an uppercut.

Automatic Take on the 3-0 Pitch

The automatic take on a 3-0 pitch is a tactic that is best used when a pitcher is struggling with his control and isn't throwing many strikes. When the batter has this count, he must not swing at the next pitch because the chances of drawing a walk greatly outweigh the chances of getting a hit.

Baserunning Strategy

For your players to be effective baserunners, they must know how, when, and why to remain at a base or try to advance. They must be aware of the strength of the outfielder's arm if they are trying to advance on a base hit or a fly ball. They must also be aware of the team's overall strategy in a given circumstance so that they know whether to be aggressive or play it safe. If your team is trailing in the late innings of a game, your runners should not take any unnecessary chances on the bases, because every baserunner becomes even more valuable in these situations. On the other hand, aggressive baserunning early in a game can often force an opponent into making mistakes and can be a positive factor for your team.

As a Babe Ruth League coach, you should teach players the following things in order to help them gain a tactical advantage when they are on base:

- Watch the pitcher prepare to pitch the ball. Once the pitcher strides toward home plate, he cannot throw to a base, so your baserunner can increase the leadoff or try to steal. However, if the pitcher steps toward first base or moves his back foot off the rubber, your runner should quickly return to the bag.

- Listen to and watch the base coach. The base coach's job is to watch what's going on in the field and help players run the bases safely. Runners on first base should listen to instructions from the first-base coach; runners on second and third base should follow the instructions of the third-base coach.

- Do not run unless you are forced to. Baserunners are not always forced to run. For example, if a runner is on first base and a fly ball is caught in the outfield, the runner is not forced to go to second and can stay at first base. The base coach should tell the baserunners when a force is in effect.

- Stay close to the base and tag up on fly balls. At younger levels, you can send runners halfway to the next base on fly balls to the outfield because about as many fly balls will be dropped as caught. However, at all levels, if a fly ball is caught, a runner who has left a base must tag up (touch the base he was occupying before the play started) before advancing.

Once players have mastered these fundamentals of baserunning strategy, the coach should introduce more specific, aggressive tactics, such as the steal, delayed steal, and double steal.

FIRST TO THIRD

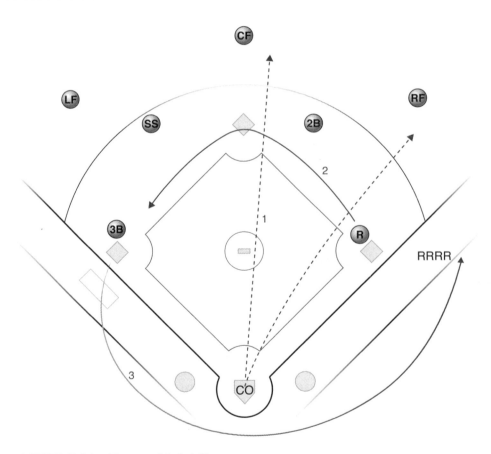

FIGURE 9.14   First to third drill.

Description

Divide the team into two groups. Play on a field appropriate for the age group, with three or four players in the outfield (use only a center fielder or use a left center fielder and right center fielder) and three more in the infield (at second base, third base, and shortstop) making up the defensive team (see figure 9.14). Depending on the size of the team, adjustments may have to be made. For the offensive team, one runner is on first base, and all remaining players in the group are lined up in foul territory near the base, waiting for their turn as the runner. For this game, a pitcher will not be necessary. The coach will act as the batter and hit fungoes from the home plate area. When the ball is hit, the runner attempts to advance from first to third base. Two points are awarded each time a runner reaches third base safely. If runners judge they cannot make it to third, they should stay at second. If the coach thinks they made the correct decision, one point is added to the score. If the coach feels the runner should have attempted to go to third and did not, a point is deducted. The defensive team is given a point for each properly executed relay throw. After each runner has had two turns, the offensive team will become the defensive team, and play continues.

Variations

- To make the game easier for runners, hit balls between the outfielders.
- To make the game easier for fielders, hit balls straight at the outfielders.
- To make the game more challenging for runners, bring the outfielders closer in.
- To make the game more challenging for fielders, divide the offensive team so that there is a line of runners at first base and at home plate. One runner attempts to go from first to third; the other goes from home plate to second base. Award the offense one point when a player reaches third base and one point if the player who starts at home plate reaches second base. Take away a point for an out recorded at either base.

Steal

To execute a steal, a baserunner takes off for the next base as the pitch is delivered, attempting to advance safely to the base before the catcher's throw arrives. When teaching runners this tactic, the coach should emphasize watching the delivery of the pitcher, getting a jump on the pitch, running hard, and sliding at the next base to avoid the tag. The steal might be a good tactic to use when a team needs to advance a runner into scoring position. It is particularly effective when the runner is fast, and it can be a good alternative when the batter is not a very good bunter. The steal can also be used to take advantage of an opposing catcher's weak throwing arm.

⟲ FAST FEET

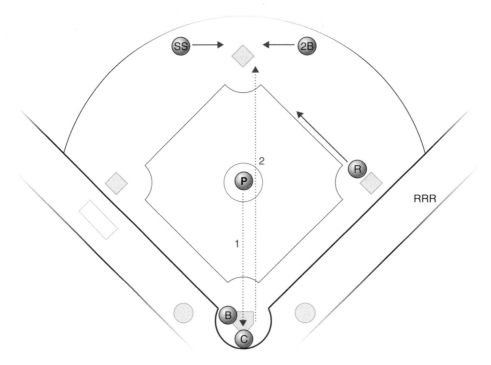

FIGURE 9.15   Fast feet drill.

Description

Play 4v4 on a field appropriate for the age group. A pitcher, catcher, second-base player, and shortstop make up the defensive team. The offensive team has a runner on first, a batter at the plate, and additional players waiting in foul territory near first base (see figure 9.15). The pitcher throws the ball, but the batter does not swing. On the pitch, the runner on first takes off for second, and the catcher attempts to throw the runner out. After the play is completed, the runner moves to foul territory and waits for his turn to run again. Play resumes when the next runner occupies first base and the pitcher prepares to pitch again. If possible, rotate catchers occasionally to avoid straining an arm. The offensive team is awarded one point for every stolen base. Rotate runners until each runner has had three steal attempts, then rotate teams and repeat.

Variations

- To make the game easier for younger or less skilled players, shorten the distance between bases.
- To make the game more challenging for older or more skilled players, make the runner wait until the ball gets to the plate.

Delayed Steal

A delayed steal is similar to the straight steal, as described previously, except the runner waits until the catcher's or the middle infielders' attention is diverted or relaxed before he starts to run. For instance, a runner may wait to take off until a catcher begins to lazily lob the ball back to the pitcher. By the time the pitcher catches the throw, the runner can be safely sliding into the base. Another opportunity to use the delayed steal is when the middle infielders do not cover second base after the pitch. The delayed steal may be a good option when the baserunner is not particularly fast or when your team needs to advance a runner into scoring position.

Double Steal

A double steal is simply a straight steal that involves two runners—one at first base and one at second. In a double-steal situation, both runners try to steal the next base on the same pitch. The defense will most likely try to make a play on the lead runner, who will be stealing third base. If successful, the double steal puts runners on second and third base, which means both runners are in scoring position (on bases from which it is possible to score if the batter gets a base hit).

Another version of the double steal can be used when runners occupy both first and third base. This double-steal play is used to try to score a run when a weak hitter is at the plate and the defense is not focused. This is known as a first and third play. The strategy in this situation calls for the runner at first (the trailing runner) to break for second base and try to draw a throw from the catcher. If this happens, the runner at third (the lead runner) then breaks quickly for home and tries to beat the throw back to the plate by the middle infielder.

Games provide the opportunity for your players to show what they've learned in practice. Just as your players' focus shifts on game days from learning and practicing to competing, your focus shifts from teaching skills to coaching players as they perform those skills in games. Of course, the game is a teaching opportunity as well, but the focus is on performing what has been learned, participating, and having fun.

In previous chapters, you learned how to teach your players techniques and tactics; in this chapter, you will learn how to coach your players as they execute those techniques and tactics in games. We provide important coaching principles that will guide you before, during, and after the game.

Before the Game

Many coaches focus on how they will coach only during the actual game, when instead preparations should begin well before the first play of the game. Ideally, a day or two before a game, you should cover several things—in addition to techniques and tactics—to prepare your players for the game. Depending on the age group you are working with, you will need to create a specific game plan for the opponent based on information that is available to you. This task will include making decisions on specific team tactics that you want to use. You should also discuss pregame particulars such as what to eat before the game, what to wear, and when to be at the field.

COACHING TIP When developing your game plan, keep in mind that your players need to understand what you expect of them during the game. You should be clear about this in the days leading up to a game. Take time at the beginning or end of each practice to discuss these expectations.

Deciding Team Tactics

Some coaches burn the midnight oil as they devise a complex plan of attack. Team tactics at this level, however, don't need to be complex—especially for the younger age groups. On offense, the focus should be on moving runners and employing smart baserunning. On defense, the focus should be on making sure of getting one out, getting the lead runner whenever possible, making good cutoffs and relays, and throwing to the proper base. You should emphasize the importance of teamwork, of every player fulfilling his role, and of every player knowing his assignments. As you become more familiar with your team's tendencies and abilities, you can help them focus on specific tactics that will help them play better. For example, if your team has a tendency to stand around and watch the action, you can emphasize moving into position to back up hits and throws. If they execute backups well but often miss the cutoff player (perhaps in trying to make too long a throw) or throw to the wrong base, you can emphasize proper positioning on cutoffs, teamwork, and communication.

During the week before a game, you should inform players of the tactics that you think will work and that you plan to use in the game. Depending on the age level, experience, and knowledge of your players, you may want to let them help you determine the tactics that you will call in the game. It is the coach's role to help youngsters grow through the sport experience. Allowing player input helps your players learn the game and involves them at a planning level often reserved

Creating a Game Plan

Just as you need a practice plan for what you will cover at each practice, you also need a game plan for game day. As a coach for youth baseball, your game plan will vary depending on the age group you are working with. As you begin planning and mapping out how your game days will progress, you should keep the following age-related points in mind.

Ages 4 to 10	• Encourage players to try their best. • Focus on helping players develop their individual skills for team competition. • Do not spend too much time just playing games, because this will cause players' skill level to be low.
Ages 11 to 12	• The strengths and weaknesses of the opposition are of little concern at this age, and the focus should be on helping your team execute the skills they have learned. • Players should concentrate on basic catching and throwing skills that make it easy for the team to execute basic defensive plays (e.g., tag plays, force plays). • Remind players of one aspect of running or hitting and one aspect of defense that they have learned that should be focused on for the game; give players a starting lineup before the first game.
Ages 13 to 18	• Players should begin to focus on one or two of the opponent's strengths and weaknesses, and they should be able to take advantage of this while the game is being played. • Teams will sometimes adjust their play based on the opponent, but the main focus is still the proper execution of the techniques and skills learned in practice. • Players should use more complex team offensive and defensive strategies (squeeze play, steal, pickoffs, and so on) that will take advantage of the opponent's weaknesses.

solely for the coach. It also gives them a feeling of ownership. Rather than just carrying out orders for the coach, they're executing the plan of attack that they helped decide. Youngsters who have a say in how they approach a task often respond with more enthusiasm and motivation.

Discussing Pregame Details

Players need to know what to do before a game, such as what they should eat on game day and when, what clothing they should wear to the game, what equipment they should bring, what time they should arrive, and how the warm-up will be run. You should discuss these particulars with them at the last practice before a game. Here are some guidelines for discussing these issues.

COACHING TIP You should have a preset plan or routine that is used before every game. This can help alleviate nerves and build confidence in your players, especially those in younger age groups. A pregame routine will also help players forget outside concerns and focus on the game.

Pregame Meal

In general, the goal for the pregame meal is to fuel the player for the upcoming event and to maximize carbohydrate stores (which are easily absorbed and are a ready source of fuel). Some foods digest more quickly than others, such as carbohydrate and protein, so we suggest that players consume these rather than fat, which digests more slowly. Good carbohydrate foods include spaghetti, rice, and bran. Good protein foods include low-fat yogurt and boneless, skinless chicken. Players should eat foods that they are familiar with and that they know they can digest easily. Big meals should be eaten three to four hours before the game. Of course, players who don't have time for a big meal can use sport beverages and meal-replacement bars instead, but these shouldn't be used regularly as a replacement for the pregame meal.

Clothing and Equipment

Depending on the age group, where the game is played, and how far the team travels to the game, you should typically require that your players wear their uniforms to the game and change into their cleats at the game site. Even T-ball teams wear uniforms today, but if your league does not provide uniforms, you should tell your players what you expect them to wear on game days. Other items that baseball players may choose to wear (but are not mandatory) include batting gloves and sliding shorts. An optional piece of equipment that is becoming more popular for younger players is the face mask attached to the batting helmet, which adds protection from thrown balls.

COACHING TIP Some coaches prefer that all players on the team wear shoes of the same type and color. For players, especially those in younger age groups, working together to pick the type and color of the shoe can be an excellent team-bonding activity (of course, you must also be sensitive to the economic environment of your players).

Arrival Time

Your players need to adequately warm up before a game, so you should instruct them to arrive 30 to 45 minutes before game time to go through the team warm-up (see the next section). You can designate where you want the team to gather as they arrive. Consider making a team rule stating that players must show up 30 to 45 minutes before a game (depending on the age group) and go through the complete team warm-up, or they won't start.

Warm-Up

Players need to both physically and mentally prepare for a game once they arrive at the field, and physical preparation involves warming up. We've suggested that players arrive 30 to 45 minutes before the game to warm up depending on the age group of your players. Even younger players who seem to be already warmed up when they get out of bed in the morning need to learn the value of a good warm-up routine. You will want to conduct the pregame warm-up similar to practice warm-ups. Before game day, you should walk the players through the steps for how they will enter and where they will line up on the field for the warm-up. The warm-up should consist of a few brief games or drills that focus on skill practice, stretching, and exercises or activities that involve a range of motion, such as throwing drills that get the players running while catching the ball.

COACHING TIP Although the site coordinator and officials have the formal responsibilities for facilities and equipment, you should know what to look for to ensure that the game is safe for all players (see Facilities and Equipment Checklist at the end of chapter 4). You should arrive at the game site earlier than your team so you can check the facility, check in with the site coordinator and officials, and greet your players as they arrive to warm up.

You should refrain from delivering a long-winded pep talk prior to the game, but you can help players mentally prepare for the game by reminding them of two or three of the skills they've been working on in recent practices and by focusing their attention on their strengths and what they've been doing well. Also take time to remind players that they should work as a team, play hard and smart, and have fun!

Communicating With Parents

The groundwork for your communication with parents will have been laid in the parent-orientation meeting, where the parents learned the best ways to support their kids'—and the whole team's—efforts on the field. You should encourage parents to judge success based not just on the outcome of the game, but also on how the kids are improving their performances.

If parents yell at the kids for mistakes made during the game, make disparaging remarks about the umpires or opponents, or shout instructions on which tactics to use, you should ask them to refrain and to instead support the team through their comments and actions. These standards of conduct should all be covered in the preseason parent-orientation meeting.

When time permits, as parents gather before a game (and before the team has approached the field), you can let them know in a general sense what the team has been focusing on during the past week and what your goals are for the game. However, your players must come first during this time, so focus on your players during the pregame warm-up.

After a game, quickly come together as a coaching staff and decide what to say to the team. Then, if the opportunity arises, you can informally assess with parents how the team did based not on the outcome, but on meeting performance goals and playing to the best of their abilities. Help parents see the game as a process, not solely as a test that is pass or fail, win or lose. Encourage parents to reinforce that concept at home.

For more information on communicating with parents, see chapter 2.

Unplanned Events

Part of being prepared to coach is to expect the unexpected. What do you do if players are late? What if *you* have an emergency and can't make the game or will be late? What if the game is rained out or otherwise postponed? Being prepared to handle out-of-the-ordinary circumstances will help you if and when unplanned events happen.

If players are late, you may have to adjust your starting lineup. Although this may not be a major inconvenience, you should stress to your players that there are important reasons for being on time. First, part of being a member of a team is being committed to and responsible for the other members. When players don't show up, or show up late, they break that commitment. And second, players need to go through a warm-up to physically prepare for the game. Skipping the warm-up risks injury.

There may be a time when an emergency causes you to be late or miss a game. In these cases, you should notify your assistant coach, if you have one, or the league coordinator. If notified in advance, a parent of a player or another volunteer might be able to step in for the game.

Sometimes a game will be postponed because of inclement weather or for other reasons, such as unsafe field conditions. If the postponement takes place before game day, you must communicate with every member of your team to let them know. If it happens while the teams are on-site and preparing for the game, you should gather your team members and explain why the game has been postponed. Make sure that all your players have a ride home before you leave—you should be the last to leave.

During the Game

Throughout the game, you must keep the game in proper perspective and help your players do the same. You should observe how your players execute techniques and tactics and how well they play together. These observations will help you decide on appropriate practice plans for the following week. Let's take a more detailed look at your responsibilities during a game.

COACHING TIP Winning games is the short-term goal of your baseball program; helping your players learn the techniques and tactics and rules of baseball, how to become fit, and how to be good sports in baseball and in life is the long-term goal. Your young players are winning when they are becoming better human beings through their participation in baseball. You have the privilege of setting the tone for how your team approaches the game. Keep winning and all aspects of the competition in proper perspective, and your young players will likely follow suit.

Tactical Decisions

Although you won't need to create a complex game strategy, as mentioned before, you will need to make tactical decisions in several areas throughout a game. You'll make decisions about who starts the game and when to enter substitutes, about making slight adjustments to your team's tactics, and about dealing with players' performance errors.

Starting and Substituting Players

For youth league baseball coaches, the task of substituting players has become decidedly more simple recently. Nearly all youth baseball associations that govern leagues for 4- to 12-year-olds have rules stipulating that each player on a roster must bat at least once during a game. Teams at this age group usually let all players on a roster bat in rotation, guaranteeing that all players get an equal opportunity to play on offense. Although not in general use, some leagues allow free substitution—which is the rule in most other sports—at any time during a game on offense or defense. If your league has no policy regarding playing time, you should make sure that everyone on the team gets to play at least half of each game. This should be your guiding principle as you consider starting and substitution patterns. For older players, the rules generally state that starting players may reenter the game once after a substitute has replaced them, provided that they occupy the same spot in the batting order. When players reach the 13- to 18-year age group, substitution becomes a much more tactical decision for the coach. See Substitutions in chapter 3 for more information on substitutions.

Adjusting Team Tactics

At the 4- to 10-year and 11- to 12-year age groups, you probably won't adjust your team tactics or plays too significantly during a game. Rather, you'll focus on the basic tactics, and during breaks in the game and between innings, you'll emphasize the specific tactics your team needs to work on. However, coaches of 13- to 18-year-olds might have reason to make tactical adjustments to improve their team's chances of performing well and winning. As games progress, assess your opponents' style of play and tactics, and make adjustments that are appropriate—that is, those that your players are prepared for. You may want to consider the following examples when adjusting team tactics:

- Does the pitcher use a high leg kick or not pay attention to baserunners? If so, you might want to have runners steal more often.

- Does the opposing team's offense revolve around a couple of key hitters? If this is the case, you might instruct your pitcher to pitch around those hitters—not give them anything good to hit.

- Is the opposing team's defense shoddy, especially in the area of cutoffs and relays? This might prompt you to advise your players to gamble on the bases more, trying to take the extra base.

- Is the opposing pitcher overpowering? You might instruct your batters to cut down on their swings, try to go to the opposite field, and even lay down a bunt or two.

Knowing the answers to such questions can help you formulate an effective game plan and make proper adjustments during a game. However, don't stress tactics too much during a game. Doing so can take the fun out of the game for the players. If you don't trust your memory, carry a pen and pad to note which team tactics and individual skills need attention at the next practice.

Correcting Players' Errors

In chapter 6, you learned about two types of errors: learning errors and performance errors. Learning errors are those that occur because players don't know how to perform a skill. Performance errors are made not because players don't know how to execute the skill but because they make mistakes in carrying out what they do know.

Sometimes it's not easy to tell which type of error players are making. Knowing your players' capabilities helps you to determine if they know the skill and are simply making mistakes in executing it or if they don't know how to perform it. If they are making learning errors—that is, they don't know how to perform the skill—you should note this and cover it at the next practice. Game time is not the time to teach skills.

If they are making performance errors, however, you can help players correct those errors during a game. Players who make performance errors often do so because they have a lapse in concentration or motivation, or they are simply demonstrating human error. Competition and contact can also adversely affect a young player's technique, and a word of encouragement about concentration may help. If you do correct a performance error during a game, do so in a quiet, controlled, and positive tone of voice during a break or when the player is on the bench with you.

For those making performance errors, you must determine if the error is just an occasional error that anyone can make or if it is an expected error for a youngster at that stage of development. If the latter is the case, then the player may appreciate your not commenting on the mistake. The player knows it was a mistake and may already know how to correct it. On the other hand, perhaps an encouraging word and a coaching cue (such as "Remember to rotate the shoulder and hip—don't bail out!") may be just what the player needs. Knowing the players and what to say is very much a part of the art of coaching.

COACHING TIP Designate an area near the team bench or dugout where players gather after coming off the field. In this area, you can speak to them either individually or as a group and make necessary adjustments.

Coach and Player Behavior

Another aspect of coaching on game day is managing behavior—both yours and your players'. As a coach, it is your responsibility to control emotions when aspects of the game, such as the pitching strategies you are using, are not working as you or your players would have hoped.

Coach Conduct

You very much influence your players' behavior before, during, and after a game. If you're up, your players are more likely to be up. If you're anxious, they'll take notice, and the anxiety can become contagious. If you're negative, they'll respond with worry. If you're positive, they'll play with more enjoyment. If you're constantly yelling instructions or commenting on mistakes and errors, it will be difficult for players to concentrate. Instead, you should let players get into the flow of the game.

The focus should be on positive competition and on having fun. A coach who over-organizes everything and dominates a game from the bench is definitely not making the game fun.

So how should you conduct yourself on the bench? Here are a few pointers:

- Be calm, in control, and supportive of your players.
- Encourage players often, but instruct during play sparingly. Players should focus on their performance during a game, not on instructions shouted from the bench.
- If you need to instruct a player, do so in an unobtrusive manner when you're both on the bench. Never yell at players for making a mistake. Instead, briefly demonstrate or remind them of the correct technique, and encourage them. Tell them how to correct the problem on the field.

You should also make certain that you have discussed bench demeanor as a coaching staff and that everyone is in agreement on the way the coaches should conduct themselves on the bench. Remember, you're not playing for an Olympic gold medal! At this level, baseball competitions are designed to help players develop their skills and themselves—and to have fun. So coach in a manner at games that helps your players achieve these things.

Player Conduct

You're responsible for keeping your players under control. Do so by setting a good example and by disciplining when necessary. Set team rules for good behavior. If players attempt to cheat, fight, argue, badger, yell disparaging remarks, and the like, it is your responsibility to correct the misbehavior. Initially, this may mean removing players immediately from the game, letting them calm down, and then speaking to them quietly, explaining that their behavior is not acceptable for your team—and that if they want to play, they must not repeat the action. You should remember, too, that younger players are still learning how to deal with their emotions in addition to learning the game. As a coach, you must strive to remain calm during times when a young player is having trouble controlling his emotions.

You should consider team rules in these areas of game conduct:

- Player language
- Player behavior
- Interactions with umpires
- Discipline for misbehavior
- Dress code for competitions

Player Welfare

All players are not the same. Some attach their self-worth to winning and losing. This idea is fueled by coaches, parents, peers, and society, who place great emphasis on winning. Players become anxious when they're uncertain whether they can meet the expectations of others—especially when meeting a particular expectation is important to them also.

If your players look uptight and anxious during a game, you should find ways to reduce both the uncertainties about how their performance will be evaluated and the importance they are attaching to the game. Help players focus on realistic personal goals—goals that are reachable and measurable and that will help them improve their performance, all while having fun as they play. Another way to reduce anxiety on game day is to stay away from emotional pregame pep talks. Instead, remind players of the techniques and tactics they will use, and remind them to play hard, to do their best, and to have fun.

When coaching during games, remember that the most important outcome from playing baseball is to build or enhance players' self-worth. Keep that firmly in mind, and strive to promote this through every coaching decision.

Keeping the Game Safe

Chapter 4 is devoted to player safety, but it's worth noting here that safety during games can be affected by how umpires call the rules. If umpires aren't calling rules correctly and this risks injury to your players, you must intervene. Voice your concern in a respectful manner and in a way that places the emphasis where it should be—on the players' safety. One of the umpires' main responsibilities is to provide for players' safety. Both you and the umpires are working together to protect the players whenever possible. Don't hesitate to address an issue of safety with an umpire when the need arises.

Opponents and Umpires

You must respect opponents and umpires. Without them, there wouldn't be a competition. Opponents provide opportunities for your team to test itself, improve, and excel. Umpires help provide a fair and safe experience for players and, as appropriate, help them learn the game.

You and your team should show respect for opponents and umpires by giving your best efforts and being civil. Don't allow your players to trash talk or taunt an opponent or an umpire. Such behavior is disrespectful to the spirit of the competition, and you should immediately remove a player from a game (as discussed previously in Player Conduct) if that player disobeys your team rules in this area.

Remember, too, that umpires at this level are quite often teenagers—in many cases not much older than the players themselves—and the level of officiating should be commensurate to the level of play. In other words, don't expect perfection from umpires any more than you do from your own players. Especially at younger levels, umpires might have a more liberal strike zone, for example, because if they didn't, each inning could last a very long time, and the pitcher would quickly become tired. As long as the calls are being made consistently on both sides, most of your officiating concerns will be alleviated.

After the Game

When the game is over, join your team in congratulating the coaches and players of the opposing team, then be sure to thank the umpires. Check on any injuries players sustained, and inform players on how to care for them. Be prepared to speak with the umpires about any problems that occurred during the game. Then hold a brief meeting to ensure that your players are on an even keel, whether they won or lost.

Reactions Following a Game

Your first concern after a game should be your players' attitudes and mental well-being. You don't want them to be too high after a win or too low after a loss. This is the time you can be most influential in keeping the outcome in perspective and keeping players on an even keel.

When celebrating a victory, make sure your team does so in a way that doesn't show disrespect for the opponents. It's okay and appropriate to be happy and celebrate a win, but don't allow your players to taunt the opponents or boast about their victory. If your team was defeated, your players will naturally be disappointed. But, if your team has made a winning effort, let them know this. After a loss, help them keep their chins up and maintain a positive attitude that will carry over into the next practice and game. Winning and losing are a part of life, not just a part of sport. If players can handle both equally well, they'll be successful in whatever they do.

Postgame Team Meeting

Following the game, gather your team in a designated area for a short meeting. Before this meeting, decide as a coaching staff what to say and who will say it. Be sure that the staff speaks with one voice following the game.

If your players have performed well in a game, you should compliment them and congratulate them. Tell them specifically what they did well, whether they won or lost. This will reinforce their desire to repeat their good performances. Don't use this time to criticize individual players for poor performances in front of teammates or attempt to go over tactical problems and adjustments. You should help players improve their skills, but do so at the next practice. Immediately after a game, players won't absorb much tactical information.

Finally, make sure your players have transportation home. Be the last one to leave to ensure full supervision of your players.

We hope you've learned a lot from this book: what your responsibilities are as a Babe Ruth League coach, how to communicate well and provide for safety, how to teach and shape skills, and how to coach on game days. But game days make up only a portion of your season—you and your players will spend more time in practices than in competition. How well you conduct practice sessions and prepare your players for competition will greatly affect not only your players' enjoyment and success throughout the season but also your own.

Fun Learning Environment

Regardless of where you are in your season, you must create an environment that welcomes learning and promotes teamwork. Following are seven tips that will help you get the most out of your practices:

1. Stick to the practice times agreed on as a staff.
2. Start and end each practice as a team.
3. Keep the practice routine as consistent as possible so that the players can feel comfortable.
4. Be organized in your approach by moving quickly from one drill to another and from one practice segment to another.
5. Tell your players what the practice will include before the practice starts.
6. Allow the players to take water breaks whenever possible.
7. Focus on providing positive feedback.

You may also want to consider using gamelike drills, such as those found in chapters 7 through 9, to make practices more fun. During your season, it may be fun to use the games toward the end of the week to add variety to your practices.

Season Plans

Your season plan acts as a snapshot of the entire season. Before the first practice with your players, you must sit down as a coaching staff and develop a season plan. To do this, simply write down each practice and game date on a calendar, and then go back and number your practices. These practice numbers will become the foundation of your season plan. Now you can work through the season plan, moving from practice to practice, to create a quick overview of what you hope to cover in each practice. You should note the purpose of the practice, the main skills you will cover, and the activities you will use during that particular practice. While developing your season plan, keep in mind that you will want to incorporate the games approach into your practices. The games approach is superior to the traditional approach because it focuses on replicating the game environment. Using gamelike drills better develops the players both physically and mentally to the demands of the game.

Following is more detailed information about season plans for each particular age group—ages 4 to 10, ages 11 to 12, and ages 13 to 18.

Season Plan for Ages 4 to 10

Many players in this age group have had little or no exposure to baseball, so you shouldn't automatically assume that they have any knowledge of the game. As a Babe Ruth League coach, you will be expected to help them explore the basic technical and tactical skills of the sport, as suggested in the following season plan.

Practice	Purpose	Related technical and tactical skills
1	To learn throwing and catching techniques	Proper grip; throwing; catching; throwing to bases
2	To defend in the infield on ground balls	Fielding grounders and throwing to first base; hitting and running to first base; running form
3	To learn hitting mechanics	Hitting off a batting tee; fielding batted balls; running to first base after hitting
4	To defend in the outfield on fly balls and ground balls	Fielding grounders and throwing to the appropriate base; fielding fly balls and throwing to the appropriate base; hitting off the tee; running the bases
5	To develop bunting techniques and baserunning skills	Bunting and running to first base; fielding bunts and throwing to first base
6	To work on hitting and baserunning mechanics and throwing	Hitting off the batting tee; running the bases; tagging up and advancing; fielding
7	To defend at second base by using force plays	Fielding ground balls; making force plays at second base; tag plays
8	To work on pitching and throwing mechanics	Pitching; hitting; throwing; running out the hits
9	To defend at third base by fielding bunts and making tag plays	Making tag plays at third base; fielding bunts; baserunning
10	To work on hitting and baserunning strategies	Hitting off the batting tee; fielding and throwing to bases; running out the hits
11	To defend in the outfield, including making relay throws	Fielding ground balls and fly balls in the outfield; throwing to a relay person; running the bases
12	To work on bat control and hitting mechanics	Hitting off the batting tee; hitting only ground balls; running the bases
13	To develop pitching and bunting skills	Pitching; bunting; running out bunts
14	To defend at second base and first base by converting double plays	Fielding grounders and throwing to second base; running the bases; making double plays

Season Plan for Ages 11 to 12

The season plan for this age group builds on the previous one (for ages 4 to 10) as players practice the fundamental technical and tactical skills. A few new strategies are also added, including defending in rundowns, defending home on balls hit to the infield, and executing the hit-and-run.

Practice	Purpose	Related technical and tactical skills
1	To learn throwing, catching, and fielding ground balls	Throwing; fielding ground balls; throwing to the appropriate base
2	To develop hitting techniques	Hitting off a batting tee; running to first base; fielding and throwing
3	To learn pitching mechanics	Pitching to each other; pitching to a batter; hitting and baserunning
4	To defend at second base on force plays	Fielding grounders and throwing to second base; covering second base; running from first to second base
5	To defend at second base and first base on double plays	Making double plays; stretching at first base
6	To learn bunting techniques and baserunning skills	Bunting; fielding bunts; baserunning; throwing to the right base; covering bases
7	To defend at third base in tag-play and force-play situations	Covering third base in force situations; catching fly balls in the outfield; tagging up and running from second to third base
8	To improve batting techniques and speed of the swing	Hitting off a tee to the follow-through side of the field; baserunning; hitting against the coach's pitching
9	To learn cutoff strategies and defend against balls hit to the outfield with a runner on first base	Fielding balls; backing up the outfielders; throwing to the cutoff player; covering bases; baserunning; cutoff player throwing to the back base
10	To defend against balls hit to the outfield with a runner on third base	Fielding fly balls in the outfield; tagging up on third base; throwing to the cutoff person; throwing to the correct base; improving throwing speed and release
11	To work on baserunning techniques and defending in a rundown situation	Covering second and third base; running from second to third base; rundown practice
12	To defend at home plate on balls hit to the infield	Covering home plate; fielding ground balls and throwing to home plate; running from third to home plate; infield playing in

Practice	Purpose	Related technical and tactical skills
13	To work on the hit-and-run	Hitting balls off the tee on the ground behind the runner; attempting to run from first to third base; fielding and throwing to the proper base
14	To improve the mechanics of pitching	Throwing to each other; throwing to a catcher; throwing to a batter (working on control, velocity, and changing speeds on the pitch)

Season Plan for Ages 13 to 18

In this age group, players are refining the skills they have learned from past years. The season plan for this age group builds on those for the two previous age groups and adds several new tactics, including stealing bases and holding runners on base.

Practice	Purpose	Related technical and tactical skills
1	To evaluate players' overall playing abilities and identify their best positions	Pitching and hitting; throwing; catching; baserunning
2	To develop fielding and hitting techniques	Fielding grounders and fly balls; throwing to first base; hitting and running to first base
3	To teach rundowns, cutoffs, and baserunning strategies	Outfielders throwing balls to second and third base; baserunning; throwing balls to relay players and to bases
4	To work on stealing bases and offensive strategies	Taking the lead and sprinting from first to second base; hitting; practicing hit-and-run situations
5	To defend in the infield on force plays at second base	Running from first to second base; fielding grounders and throwing to second base for force plays
6	To work on pitching techniques and strategies	Pitching to a catcher; throwing to a batter; holding runners on base
7	To advance baserunners from second to third base	Bunting; baserunning; hitting behind the runner
8	To defend in the infield on tag plays at home plate	Covering home plate on tag plays; baserunning; bunts
9	To convert double plays from second base to first base	Double-play pivots; quickness of the throw; baserunning
10	To work on offensive strategies, in particular the hit-and-run	Hitting behind the runner; advancing from first to third base

> continued

Season Plan for Ages 13 to 18 > *continued*

11	To defend on balls hit to the outfield with a runner on second base	Fielding in the outfield; backing up the out-fielder; covering third base and home plate; cutoff throws; baserunning
12	To improve pitching techniques and strategies	Pitching (control, velocity); holding runners on base; hitting
13	To develop bat control, speed, and contact	Hitting off a batting tee; hitting against live pitching
14	To increase baserunning skills and strategies	Taking leads; advancing from first to third base; attempting to steal second base in a game situation; tagging up at third base on fly balls

Practice Plans

Coaches rarely believe they have enough time to practice everything they want to cover. To help organize your thoughts and help you stay on track toward your practice objectives, you should create practice plans. These plans help you better visualize and prepare so that you can run your practices effectively.

First and foremost, your practice plans should be age appropriate for the age group you are coaching. The plans should incorporate all of the skills and concepts presented in the particular age group's season plan. To begin, each practice plan should note the practice objective (which is drawn from your season plan) and the equipment necessary to execute the specific activities in the practice. Each practice plan should also include a warm-up and cool-down. During the cool-down, coaches should attend to any injuries suffered during practice and make sure that the players drink plenty of water. It is also a good idea to have the players loosen their shoelaces to help the circulation in the feet.

SAMPLE PRACTICE PLAN FOR AGES 4 TO 10

Objective

To learn basic hitting mechanics; to continue learning throwing and catching skills

Equipment

Rag balls, safety balls, extra gloves, bats, batting tees, fungo bat, helmets, catcher gear

ACTIVITY	DESCRIPTION	COACHING POINTS
Pre-practice meeting (5 min.)	The coach takes roll call. The coach explains the purpose of the practice: to improve hitting skills.	• Make eye contact with every player
Warm-up (10 min.)	Players jog once around the perimeter of the field and then assemble in a circle around the coach. The coach demonstrates basic stretches, and the players perform the stretches; after stretching, the players run a series of sprints.	• Loosening up muscles • Improving core body strength • Improving agility and balance • Improving reflexes • Preparing muscles for hitting
Throwing (10 min.)	Players perform the Throwing Drill as described on page 99. Coaches circulate among the players, correcting, demonstrating, and praising throwing techniques.	• Emphasize proper grip • Using overhand throwing action • Keeping elbow above shoulder at top of arc • Using proper follow-through • Rotating upper body on throw
Catching (5 min.)	The team performs the Catching Throws Drill as described on page 102. Coaches throw to players. Coaches provide feedback on technique to each player.	• Keeping chest in front of ball • Catching ball while stepping toward it with the throwing-side foot • Using two hands
Throwing and catching (10 min.)	Players pair up and divide into two lines, 30 feet apart from each other. Each pair has a ball (safety ball). On the coach's command, the players with the balls execute proper throwing technique and throw to their partners. Partners execute proper catching form. After catching the ball, the players wait for the command from the coach and then throw back to their partner. Repeat 15 to 20 times. Coaches walk around the outside of the throwing area and observe, praise, and correct the players.	• Putting it all together: catching and throwing

> continued

ACTIVITY	DESCRIPTION	COACHING POINTS
Fielding practice (10 min.)	The team performs the Fielding Ground Balls Drill as described on page 108. Coaches split between the groups.	• Assuming ready position • Using proper footwork • Getting into good fielding position • Funneling the ball • Using the skip-and-throw technique
Four-Count Hitting Drill (5-10 min.)	Players line up in three or four lines facing the coach; one coach gives commands to the players, who perform the Four-Count Hitting Drill as described on page 137 without a bat. The players stand with hands on hips initially, isolating the lower body; then they assume the batting stance (without the bat) and fake the swing. Coaches circulate among the players, watching swings and commenting on skills.	• Watch grip • Check balance in stance position • Emphasize proper stride and coil • Emphasize good swing technique • Watch for overstriding
Game: Hitting Down (20 min.)	Play the Hitting Down game as described on page 145. This game stresses proper swing mechanics. Divide players into two teams. Four players are in the field on defense; substitutions should be made as necessary to give all players equal time. The coach should modify the rules to fit the age group and should explain the rules to the players. All players on the team at bat get to hit in order. Once everyone has hit, the teams switch sides so the team on defense becomes the team at bat. Play three innings. Reward the winning team.	• Emphasize hitting down • Getting out of the box • Using proper running form to first base • Fielding and throwing to first base • Making force plays • Teamwork
Cool-down (5 min.)	Players pair up and divide into two lines; each pair has a ball. Players in line A assume proper fielding position. Players in line B roll the ball underhand to their partner, trying to roll the ball into the glove. Repeat as necessary. Make a game out of it to increase accuracy and proper fielding technique. After 10 rolls each, the players perform some stretching.	• Lowering heart rate and body temperature • Repetition of fielding position • Maintaining balance

SAMPLE PRACTICE PLAN FOR AGES 11 TO 12

Objective

To teach cutoff and relay techniques and tactics; to teach aggressive baserunning; to reinforce throwing and catching skills

Equipment

Baseballs, safety balls, bats, extra gloves, batting tees, sock hitting net, helmets, orange cones, fungo bat, catcher gear

ACTIVITY	DESCRIPTION	COACHING POINTS
Pre-practice meeting (5 min.)	The coach takes roll call, reviews the previous practice (positives, negatives), and explains the purpose of today's practice: improving outfield defense and learning cutoff strategies.	• Make eye contact with every player • Single out good performances • Mention players by name who improved in previous day's work
Warm-up (20 min.)	Players jog twice around the field, perform drills to work on running form (sprints, high leg kicks, cariocas, skipping, running backward), and perform stretches and plyometrics drills.	• Increasing circulation • Loosening muscles • Improving coordination • Improving strength • Improving reflexes
Throwing (15 min.)	Players perform the Throwing Drill as described on page 99 where they pair up and play catch with each other in a yoga-style position without gloves. Then, they move into a kneeling position with their throwing-side knee on the ground and their glove-side foot pointing at their partner (increase the distance between partners to 20 feet); the players now wear gloves as they play catch, going through the proper arm motion. After 10 to 15 throws, they increase the distance to 30 feet and play catch while standing up, using complete range of motion and proper footwork. Repeat for 5 minutes. Gradually have the players move back to 45 feet. Coaches circulate among the players and provide feedback to individual players.	• Using overhand throwing motion • Catching with two hands • Keeping chest in front of ball • Catching ball while stepping toward it with the throwing-side foot
Game: On the Fly (20 min.)	Play On the Fly as described on page 129. Divide the team in half, and go through three or four of the game's variations. The coach hits balls to the fielders. After 5 balls, switch sides so the defensive team becomes the offense (baserunners). Play three or four innings depending on time. The coach should freeze play and comment when necessary.	• Proper fielding form for outfielders • Reexplain rules on tagging up and when to run • Making appropriate decisions and throwing to correct base • Using proper running form • Tagging up • Runner's ability to judge if a ball is going to be caught

> continued

ACTIVITY	DESCRIPTION	COACHING POINTS
Batting practice (20 min.)	Coaches set up stations: one batter, one on-deck hitter hitting balls off a tee into a net behind the backstop, one player feeding the tee, and one player shagging balls for the coach. All players have a number that determines batting sequence. The coach pitches to the batter. All other players are in the field fielding batted balls. Players get 5 to 10 swings, then rotate. The player who is batting runs out his last swing, remains on base and reacts to the hits of the succeeding batter until he reaches third base, then puts on his glove and moves into the field. Other coaches observe and supervise baserunning, hitting, fielding, and the players at the tee. Fielders play every ball as if it is a live ball in a game. Coaches should freeze the action when necessary.	• Proper hitting technique • Knowledge of strike zone • When to advance as a runner (and when not to) • Proper fielding technique
Game: First to Third (15 min.)	Play First to Third as described on page 150. Divide players into the same teams as used previously in the On the Fly game. The coach hits balls to right field and center field, and runners try to advance. Coaches should freeze play when necessary. Use variations as described, and shape the game to fit the runners and fielders.	• Emphasize aggressive baserunning • Emphasize making good baserunning judgments • Emphasize proper use of the crow hop • Using overhand throwing technique • Executing tag plays • Making cutoffs
Cool-down (5 min.)	Players pair up and toss easy fly balls to each other underhand. One player stands in proper position to field a fly ball; his partner tries to toss the ball into the glove.	• Lowering heart rate and body temperature • Consistent repetition

SAMPLE PRACTICE PLAN FOR AGES 13 TO 18

Objective
To begin to teach situational hitting; to emphasize aggressive baserunning strategies

Equipment
Baseballs, bats, fungo bat, orange cones, sock hitting net, batting tees, throw-down bases, helmets, catcher gear, stopwatch

ACTIVITY	DESCRIPTION	COACHING POINTS
Pre-practice meeting (5 min.)	The coach takes roll call, reviews the previous practice (positives, negatives), and explains the purpose of today's practice: working on base stealing and becoming familiar with offensive strategy, specifically the importance of the hit-and-run play.	• Make eye contact with every player • Single out good performances • Mention players by name who improved in previous day's work
Warm-up (20 min.)	Players jog twice around the field, perform drills to work on running form (sprints, high leg kicks, cariocas, skipping, running backward), and perform stretches and plyometrics drills.	• Increasing circulation • Loosening muscles • Improving coordination • Improving strength • Improving reflexes
Throwing (10-15 min.)	Players perform the Throwing Drill as described on page 99 where they pair up and play catch with each other in a yoga-style position without gloves. They progress to throwing from one knee, then throwing while standing up. Gradually increase the throwing distance to include long tosses from 150 feet away. From the longest distance, players should throw to their partner on one bounce so they don't have a "rainbow" arc throw. Coaches circulate among players and provide feedback.	• Emphasize grip • Using proper footwork • Using proper arm action • Following through on long tosses
Fielding ground balls and fly balls (20 min.)	Players divide into two groups: infielders and outfielders. Coaches split between stations. The infielders perform the Fielding Ground Balls Drill (page 108), and the outfielders perform the Fielding Fly Balls Drill (page 110). The drills are split into two parts. For the first part, the coaches throw ground balls or fly balls; for the second half of the drill, coaches should hit balls to fielders. Assign rotating players to catch for the coach.	• Using proper fielding form • Transitioning into throwing form after fielding • Hustle
Game: Fast Feet (10 min.)	Play Fast Feet as described on page 152. Divide players into teams and play 4v4; rotate players in and out of the game as needed. After each player has run once, runners and defenders should switch roles. Play two or three innings. Reward the winning team with extra swings in batting practice.	• Make positive comments • Getting a jump • Using proper sliding technique • Catcher quickness • Covering a base on a steal

> continued

Sample Practice Plan for Ages 13 to 18 > *continued*

ACTIVITY	DESCRIPTION	COACHING POINTS
Batting practice and pitching drills (20 min.)	Coaches set up stations: one batter, one on-deck hitter hitting balls off a tee into a net behind the backstop, one player feeding the tee, and one player shagging balls for the coach. All players have a number that determines batting sequence. The coach pitches to the batter. All other players are in the field fielding batted balls. Players get 5 to 10 swings, then rotate. The player who is batting runs out his last swing, remains on base and reacts to the hits of the succeeding batter until he reaches third base, then puts on his glove and moves into the field. Other coaches observe and supervise baserunning, hitting, fielding, and the players at the tee. Fielders play every ball as if it is a live ball in a game. Coaches should freeze the action when necessary. Pitchers will be working on mechanics on the sideline with a coach. They should perform the Pitcher's Balance Drill as described on page 89.	• Stress hitting mechanics • Work on hitting down off tees • Emphasize aggressive base-running • Stress good fielding position on batted balls • Assuming ready position on pitch • Using proper throwing action • Throwing back-side hip at catcher • Using proper follow-through on throws
Game: Hit-and-Run (15 min.)	Play Hit-and-Run as described on page 147. Divide the team into groups of three players each; each group of three will play against the other two groups. The coach should explain the importance of being able to advance baserunners into scoring position. Coaches should explain the rules of the game and should freeze and shape play as necessary.	• Leading with the hands on the swing • Hitting the ball down • Hitting behind the runner • Making good judgments on the bases • Throwing to the right base
Cool-down (5 min.)	Players jog around the infield perimeter twice; after each circuit, they stretch for a half minute.	• Lowering heart rate and body temperature • Using proper running form
Team meeting	The coach reviews the positives from the day's practice and inspires players for the next practice.	• Make eye contact with each player • Mention players by name who made improvements

Constructing practice plans requires both organization and flexibility on your part. Don't be intimidated by the amount of material you've listed in your season plan as skills and tactics you want to cover. Pick out a few basics and build your initial practice plans around them; this process will get easier after you've drafted a few plans. Then you can move from teaching simple concepts and skills to drawing up plans that introduce more complex ones. Build in some flexibility; if you find that what you've planned for practice isn't working, you should have a backup activity that approaches the skill or concept from a different angle. The top priorities are to keep your team playing the game and to help everyone have fun while they're learning.

Glossary

balk—An illegal motion by the pitcher resulting in a dead ball and runners advancing one base.

ball—A pitch that the batter doesn't swing at and that is outside of the strike zone.

baserunner—An offensive player who is either on base or attempting to reach a base.

batter's box—Rectangles on either side of home plate designating the area in which a batter must stand.

batting rules—A batter cannot leave the batter's box once the pitcher becomes set or begins the windup. Both feet must be inside the batter's box (the lines are part of the box). If the batter hits the ball—either fair or foul—with one or both feet on the ground entirely outside of the box, the batter is automatically out. Also, a batter may request time, but the umpire does not have to grant the request. If a batter refuses to take position in the batter's box, the umpire will order the pitcher to pitch and will call each pitch a strike, no matter the location.

bunt—A method of hitting accomplished by holding the bat so that the pitch is hit softly, traveling several feet in front of home plate or down the first- or third-base line. Players can bunt for base hits or to advance a runner into scoring position. Batters attempting to bunt on the third strike are out if the ball is not hit fair. This play is considered a strikeout.

choking up—Moving both hands up the bat handle from the knob to increase bat control.

count—The number of balls and strikes on a hitter.

crow hop—A jumping movement of the lower body used when throwing long distances to generate maximum velocity on the throw.

defensive obstruction—The baseline belongs to the runner. A fielder not in the act of fielding cannot block the path of the runner between any bases. In such a case, the ball is dead and the runner is awarded the base he would have reached, in the umpire's judgment, had he not been obstructed.

double—A hit that allows the batter to reach second base safely.

double play—A defensive play that results in putting two players out.

dropped third strike—If first base is unoccupied, or if it is occupied with two outs, and the catcher drops a third strike, the defensive team must put out the batter by either throwing to first before the batter reaches the base or by tagging the batter with the ball before he reaches first.

error—A defensive mistake that enables a runner to advance or reach a base safely that the player would otherwise have been unable to advance to or would have been put out before reaching.

fair territory—The area of the playing field between (and including) the foul lines.

fielder's choice—A situation that allows a batter to reach a base safely because a fielder decides to attempt to put out a different baserunner.

fly ball—A hit that sails high into the air; also known as a pop fly.

fly-out—A fly ball that is caught, resulting in the batter being put out.

force play—Occurs when a runner is forced to advance to the next base because the batter becomes a runner and the preceding base is occupied. On a ground ball, runners are forced to run in these situations: first base occupied; first and second occupied; first, second, and third occupied; first and third occupied (only the runner on first is forced to run). On force plays, the defender needs to touch the base while in possession of the ball before the runner reaches the base to record an out. An out resulting from a force play is called a force-out.

foul ball—Any ball hit into foul territory. Note, though, that a ground ball that is fair as it passes first or third base and then rolls into foul territory is a fair ball.

foul line—Either of the two straight lines extending at right angles from the rear of home plate through the outer edges of first and third bases to the outfield boundary. A batted ball that lands on a foul line is considered to have landed in fair territory.

foul territory—The area of the playing field that lies beyond the foul lines.

foul tip—A ball that is tipped by the batter and either caught or dropped by the catcher. With two strikes on the batter, a foul tip must be caught by the catcher for an out (a strikeout) to be recorded; otherwise the batter may still bat.

ground ball—A hit that bounces or rolls along the ground; also known as a grounder.

ground-out—A ground ball that is fielded by an infielder, resulting in the batter being put out at first base.

hit by a pitch—When a pitched ball hits any part of a batter's uniform or person, the batter has been hit by a pitch and is awarded first base. This does not count as a time at bat.

home run—A home run is recorded when a batter hits a fair ball over the fence or circles the bases on an inside-the-park hit without being thrown out.

infield—The part of the playing field enclosed by the three bases and home plate.

infield fly rule—This rule prohibits a player from intentionally dropping a fair fly ball that can be caught in the infield with normal effort. This rule is only in effect with runners on first and second, or first, second, and third, with less than two outs. When an umpire calls an infield fly rule, the batter is automatically out and runners may advance at their own risk.

inning—A division of a game that consists of each team having a turn at bat.

offensive interference—A runner is out if he intentionally interferes with a thrown ball, hinders a fielder from making a play on a batted ball, or intentionally interferes with a fielder or the ball in trying to break up a double play. In this case, both the runner and the batter are out.

out—An out can be recorded in a variety of ways, including strikeout, force-out, tag-out, and fly-out.

outfield—The part of the playing field outside the infield and between the foul lines.

overthrow—When a base is overthrown and the ball goes out of play (such as over a fence or in a dugout), runners are awarded the next base.

passed ball—A pitch not hit by the batter that passes the catcher and should have been caught (*see* wild pitch). Typically, passed balls pass the catcher in the air before bouncing. To be a passed ball, a baserunner must advance on the play.

pitching rules—With a runner or runners on base, once a pitcher begins the pitching motion to home, he must throw or he will be called for a balk. With the bases empty, a pitcher has 20 seconds to pitch or the umpire will automatically call a ball. A ball is also called for bringing the pitching hand into contact with the mouth or lips while on the mound (exceptions may be made in cold weather); for applying a foreign substance to the ball; for spitting on the ball, either hand, or the glove; and for rubbing the ball on the glove, body, or clothing. The pitcher may rub the ball in his bare hands while not in contact with the rubber. Pitchers cannot intentionally throw at a batter. Usually, a manager or coach may make two visits to the mound during an inning to talk to the pitcher; on the second trip, the pitcher must be removed. Rules on visits may vary by organization or age group.

put-out—A batter-runner or baserunner is called out (such as with a force-out or tag-out).

run—The basic unit of scoring that is credited each time a baserunner advances safely to home plate.

run batted in (RBI)—A run that scores as the direct result of the batter's action.

running out of the baseline—A runner is out when running out of the baseline, which is more than three feet away from a direct line between the bases, unless the runner does so to avoid interfering with a fielder fielding a batted ball.

running past first base—Runners are entitled to run past first base without risking being tagged out. They give up this right if they make an attempt to run toward second base, however. Once they do this, they can be tagged out.

sacrifice bunt—A bunt that results in the baserunner (or baserunners) advancing and the batter being put out.

sacrifice fly—A fly-out that results in a run being scored.

scoring position—Second or third base, from which a baserunner could score on a base hit.

single—A hit that allows the batter to reach first base safely.

squeeze play—A sacrifice bunt that occurs when a runner occupies third base. The batter bunts, and the runner safely scores on the play.

strike—A pitch that the batter doesn't swing at (takes) in the strike zone, that the batter swings at and misses, or that the batter hits into foul territory with less than two strikes.

strikeout—A batter being put out as the result of a third strike during an at-bat (either swinging and missing at a third strike or having a third strike called).

strike zone—The area over home plate through which a pitch must pass to be called a strike, between the top of the knees and the midpoint between the top of the shoulders and the top of the pants.

tag play—Occurs when a runner is not forced to advance (see force play). When a runner is not forced to advance, such as with a runner on second, the runner must be tagged out (touched with the ball, which can be in a fielder's glove or bare hand) when the runner is not touching a base.

tag up—The action of a baserunner making contact with a base after a fly ball has been caught, with the intention of advancing to the next base. A runner cannot advance to the next base on a caught fly ball until the fly ball is caught and the runner has tagged up.

triple—A hit that allows the batter to reach third base safely.

triple play—A defensive play that results in putting three players out.

walk—A batter advancing to first base as the result of having a fourth ball called. Also called a base on balls.

wild pitch—A pitch not hit by the batter that passes the catcher and could not have been caught (*see* passed ball). Typically, wild pitches are those that are in the dirt before they pass the catcher. To be considered a wild pitch, a baserunner must advance on the play.

About Babe Ruth League

Babe Ruth League, Inc. is a nonprofit, educational organization dedicated to serving all youth. In all aspects, Babe Ruth League is committed to providing our participants the very best educational sports experience possible. It is our fundamental belief that every child with a desire to play baseball or softball be afforded that opportunity.

The primary emphasis of Babe Ruth League is on the local league season and providing education, skill development, and participation for all players at all levels of athletic ability, while ensuring the participants have FUN.

Leagues chartered with Babe Ruth League operate with simplicity, democracy, and much autonomy within the framework of Babe Ruth League, Inc. rules and regulations. Babe Ruth League places no undue restrictions on local leagues, a fact that sets it far apart from all other programs.

The highlight of Babe Ruth League is its annual tournament trail. Tournament teams from each local league are eligible to participate in district, state, and regional tournaments. The winners advance to one of the Babe Ruth Baseball World Series, Babe Ruth Softball World Series, or Cal Ripken Baseball World Series.

For more information, visit www.baberuthleague.org.

Find more outstanding resources at

www.HumanKinetics.com

In the **U.S.** call 1-800-747-4457
Canada 1-800-465-7301
U.K./Europe +44 (0) 113 255 5665
International 1-217-351-5076

eBook
available at
HumanKinetics.com

 HUMAN KINETICS